NATIVE PLANTS
for Florida Gardens

STACEY MATRAZZO
AND NANCY BISSETT

FLORIDA
WILDFLOWER
FOUNDATION

Pineapple Press
West Palm Beach, Florida

 Pineapple Press

An imprint of The Rowman & Littlefield Publishing Group, Inc.
4501 Forbes Blvd., Ste. 200
Lanham, MD 20706
www.rowman.com

Distributed by NATIONAL BOOK NETWORK

British Library Cataloguing in Publication Information available

Library of Congress Cataloging-in-Publication Data available

ISBN 978-1-4930-4378-1 (paperback)
ISBN 978-1-4930-4379-8 (e-book)

♾™ The paper used in this publication meets the minimum requirements of American National
Standard for Information Sciences—Permanence of Paper for Printed Library Materials, ANSI/
NISO Z39.48-1992

CONTENTS

INTRODUCTION

When most people think of Florida, they think of sunshine, palm trees, and sandy beaches. But take another look and you'll see the state is home to an incredible array of flora and fauna and a wide range of biological communities. In fact, Florida is one of the most diverse states in the country, with more than 4,100 plant species documented, including more ancient species and families of plants than any other state.

WHY NATIVE?

Native plants are paramount to healthy ecosystems. In both natural and urban landscapes, they provide vital food and cover for native wildlife, enrich soil and control erosion, sequester carbon, reduce air and water pollution, and help maintain a healthy environment.

What makes a plant "native"? In general, a native plant is any species indigenous to or naturally occurring (without human intervention) in a particular region. In Florida, native plants are further designated as species that were present at the time of European colonization. This period marks the genesis of the state's changing landscape, when land was cleared for settlement and new species from around the world were beginning to be introduced. It is also when our first botanical records were created.

Florida has about 2,800 native plant species, which have acclimated to our state's unique soil and climate conditions over thousands of years. They have evolved adaptations that help them endure drought, salt, hurricane winds, and seasonal climate fluctuations, making them better suited than nonnative species for survival in Florida's harsh environments.

Native plants can transform your landscape into a living ecosystem. As Florida's natural lands succumb to increasing development, a thriving urban habitat can serve as a necessary connector between fragmented natural areas, creating pathways for birds, pollinators, and other animals. Even the smallest native garden can provide essential resources for wildlife. With native plants, your landscape can be more than just a pretty face. It can provide ornamental beauty that also supports wildlife and a healthy environment.

Invasive Species

Exotic species are those that have been intentionally or inadvertently introduced to areas outside their natural ranges. Exotics whose populations have aggressively expanded into natural areas due to the absence of natural controls are considered invasive. These species disrupt natural communities and displace or even eliminate native plant populations. They contribute to an overall decrease in biodiversity and ultimately diminish the quality of habitat to wildlife.

More than 1,300 exotic species have been documented in Florida. Of those, 80 are classified as Category I invasives by the Florida Exotic Pest Plant Council (FLEPPC), meaning they have altered native plant communities by changing community structures or ecological functions, or hybridizing with natives. Another 89 exotic species are listed as Category II invasives, meaning they have increased in abundance and pose an imminent threat to native communities.

Unfortunately, many listed invasive species are readily available at garden centers or as components of seed mixes. When purchasing plants, it's important to ask about the plant's origin or to visit a native plant nursery or retail center to ensure the plant's nativity. When purchasing seeds, look for and request local ecotypes propagated from responsibly collected seeds.

Resources

- To find a native nursery in your area, visit PlantRealFlorida.org.
- To purchase native wildflower seeds, visit FloridaWildflowers.com.
- For more information on invasive species in Florida, visit FLEPPC.org.
- For information on Florida's native wildflowers, visit FlaWildflowers.org.

RIGHT PLANT, RIGHT PLACE

The key to a healthy, thriving native landscape is plant selection. Choosing plants that are naturally suited to your location's light, soil, and moisture conditions will help ensure success and reduce maintenance requirements. The right plant used in the right place will establish quickly and develop a strong root system, enabling it to survive with little effort on your part.

Before selecting plants, evaluate your site's light conditions as well as soil moisture and composition. With this information, you can group plants according to similar light and moisture requirements to simplify maintenance.

How much sunlight does your planting area get throughout the day? If it receives more than six hours, consider plants that prefer full sun. Spots receiving four to six hours of sunlight are appropriate for plants that favor partial shade, while less than four hours of sunlight is suitable for shade-tolerant plants.

Is the soil typically dry, wet, or somewhere in between? Is it sandy and well-drained, or is it rich with organic matter? It is also helpful to know your soil's pH and nutrients. (If you are unsure, your county extension office can test a soil sample.) Drought tolerant plants will do well in dry, well-drained sandy soils but may experience root rot if the soil remains too moist. Choose plants adapted to wet soils for areas with poor drainage. Too much or too little sun and water can put undue stress on a plant.

Also consider the plant's growth habit and intended use. Most plants, especially shrubs and trees, are not full grown when purchased. Consider a plant's potential height and width, and give it the space it needs to mature. To create a screen or buffer, select shrubs or small trees that can be planted close together. If your goal is to establish a groundcover, select species that have a low growth habit and readily spread on their own. Many native plants can be trimmed or mowed to maintain a desired size or shape, but choosing plants according to their size and use can mean less maintenance in the end.

For year-round interest, select plants for seasonal, color, and functional diversity. Choose plants that bloom and produce fruit (seed) in different seasons to provide food for wildlife throughout the year. Add wildflowers in a variety of bloom colors and plant in masses to maximize visibility. Include host and nectar plants to attract butterflies, bees, and other beneficial insects.

Finally, know your zone. Hardiness zones indicate the area in which a plant is most likely to thrive. Select plants that are appropriate for the zone in which you live. Plants used outside their natural hardiness zone may not perform as well as they do in their natural regions.

Although many of Florida's native species also occur well outside the state borders, plants grown from stock originating elsewhere may not perform as well in your landscape as those grown from Florida ecotypes. For example, the natural range of Butterflyweed (*Asclepias tuberosa*) extends north into Canada and west to Texas, Colorado, and Minnesota. Plants from these regions, however, have evolved in very different soil, light, and climate conditions and may not thrive in Florida's harsh environments like the species' native ecotype would.

WHAT TO EXPECT FROM YOUR NATIVE GARDEN

With native plants in your landscape, you will undoubtedly see a change in activity. You may notice birds harvesting berries and seeds from trees, shrubs, and wildflowers or grabbing a tasty bug to take back to the nest. You'll see butterflies nectaring on wildflowers and laying eggs on host plants like milkweed and passionvine. Sightings of native bees, dragonflies, honeybees, and beneficial beetles and spiders also will increase. Small mammals, lizards, and other critters may make appearances. Take satisfaction in such visits—your landscape is now a living, functioning ecosystem!

You'll also notice that, unlike many sterile lawn-dominated landscapes, your native garden has seasons. Different wildflowers bloom and set seed throughout the growing season; fruits left on branches fall to the ground, bringing the next season's sprouts. Some of your native shrubs and trees may lose their leaves in the fall as daylight diminishes.

Consider enhancing your landscape for wildlife use by adding a water feature, birdhouse, or bee box. If you have well-drained soil, leave open areas for ground-nesting insects. Don't be overzealous about maintenance and cleanup. Brush piles, stumps, bunchgrasses, and plants with hollow stems may be used as cover or for nesting. When you spot chewed leaves, nix pesticide use and rejoice in the fact that your native plants are feeding the insects that make up the ground floor of the earth's complex food web. Cut or collect spent wildflower blooms when seeds have ripened to sow next season, or just pinch off old blooms, letting seeds drop where they will. Let leaves fall where they may—they provide a no-cost mulch that decomposes to replenish soil, nourishing your plants.

However, don't use "going native" as an excuse to let your landscape go. You'll no doubt trade pushing a lawnmower for weeding and pruning. Enjoy time spent on your new low-carbon maintenance activities by taking a cherished moment or two to note the new life around you.

GET GROWING!

SELECTION

It may take a while to understand your landscape's soil and drainage conditions. If your native plants don't succeed, try again, maybe with different species. Remember, success depends on using the right plant in the right place.

WATER

Water plants thoroughly when planting, then water as needed until they are established and producing new foliage. Once established, irrigate them only when needed during extended dry periods. Learn to recognize when plants look wilted and water them then. Over-irrigation can cause fungus and rot, which can kill plants. It also can cause them to grow too quickly, making them susceptible to pests and diseases, or too tall, requiring staking.

FERTILIZER

Native plants should not need fertilizer. Like overwatering, using fertilizer can cause plants to grow too quickly. Fertilizing also encourages weeds, which may outcompete wildflowers and small plants. Fertilizer is also high in nitrogen and phosphorus content, and its runoff pollutes our waterways, leading to an excess of algae and a loss of oxygen that is detrimental to fish and other aquatic wildlife. Instead, use compost or organic mulches to enhance soil when needed to encourage healthy plant growth.

SUSTAINING WILDFLOWERS

If you want wildflowers to persist on their own in the landscape, allow for self-seeding, especially for annual or short-lived species. Keep open, lightly mulched areas available for seed to germinate. You also can collect seed and plant it where you want it. When seeds germinate, you'll need to recognize wildflower sprouts so you don't remove them when weeding. To download a PDF document showing some common wildflower seedlings, visit www.flawildflowers.org/learn.

Many wildflowers are deciduous, dying back in the winter, particularly in colder areas of the state. Don't plant over them before they resprout in the spring, and don't weed them out when they sprout. Mark areas with deciduous plants so you can be on the lookout for their seasonal comeback.

MULCH

When planting, we recommend using Florida pine straw or leaf litter. To help prevent weed germination in the first month or two after planting, you can apply a 2- to 4-inch layer of mulch, but keep it away from the base of the plants. Once plants are established and before they fully flower, carefully reduce the mulch to a thin layer. Too much mulch can contribute to fungal and rot problems. To promote self-seeding of wildflowers and native plants, spread pine straw thinly enough so that you can see the soil below.

HARDINESS ZONES

The hardiness zone map can help gardeners determine which plants are most likely to thrive in their landscape. The map is based on the average annual minimum winter temperature. It is not precise.

Information on hardiness zones is included for each species.

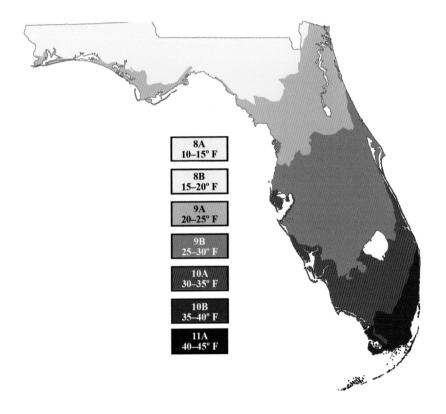

8A
10–15° F

8B
15–20° F

9A
20–25° F

9B
25–30° F

10A
30–35° F

10B
35–40° F

11A
40–45° F

QUICK-REFERENCE KEY

Look for these symbols to help you select plants that are suitable for your geographic location, soil, and light conditions. They will also help you choose plants based on other factors such as color and season of bloom.

BLOOM COLOR

White   Orange   Blue   Pink   Yellow

Purple   Red   Green   Brown

Use this color key as a general guide; exact colors of blooms will vary.

BLOOM SEASON

Winter   Spring   Summer   Fall

EXPOSURE

Full Sun   Part Sun/Shade   Full Shade

SOIL MOISTURE

Tolerates dry soil conditions   Tolerates dry to moist soils   Adapted for wet soils

HABIT

This is the average height of a mature plant.

Wildflowers

ADDING NATIVE WILDFLOWERS to your landscape can create a pleasing aesthetic while providing natural resources for wildlife. Wildflowers are critical for nourishing pollinators and act as host plants for emerging larvae. Birds savor those insects as well as wildflower seeds. Butterflies, bees, wasps, flies, and other beneficial insects visit wildflowers for nectar and pollen. Some even use hollow stems as nesting sites. Group wildflowers to add a mosaic of color and texture to your landscape.

HAMMOCK SNAKEROOT
(Ageratina jucunda)

2–3 ft.

Hammock snakeroot is a low growing, herbaceous perennial with a woody base. It is found in sandhills, dry pinelands, hammocks, and upland mixed woodlands throughout Florida's peninsula and eastern Panhandle. Its blooms attract a variety of butterflies, including hairstreaks, Julias, skippers, and crescents. Bees and hummingbirds like it, too, but the plant is poisonous to both humans and livestock if ingested.

Like other members of the Eupatorieae tribe of the aster family, Hammock snakeroot's flowers have no ray florets—only disk florets are present. They are white, tubular, and born in flat-topped clusters on branched stems. Leaves are petiolate and deltoid to narrowly rhombic with serrate margins. They are oppositely arranged and often drooping.

The species epithet *jucunda* is from the Latin *jucundus*, which means "pleasing" or "delightful." Perhaps that's because the sprinkling of its blooms looks like a fairy dusted the landscape.

FAMILY: Asteraceae (aster, composite, or daisy family)

NATIVE RANGE: Eastern Panhandle and throughout peninsular Florida

LIFESPAN: Perennial

BLOOM SEASON: Late summer through early winter

GROWTH HABIT: 2–3' tall; usually taller than wide

PROPAGATION: Hammock snakeroot easily germinates from seed and can germinate in the landscape during the winter months if moisture is adequate. Let the seed ripen and fall naturally or harvest to plant in other areas.

PLANTING: Plants are generally available in 1-gallon containers. Find spaces in well-drained soils either alone or mixed with other plants in a naturalistic planting. A 24-inch spacing is adequate.

CARE: As in all well-drained soils, plants may suffer through extended spring droughts. After blooming in the fall, they may look ragged; plants may be trimmed back any time before spring to give a fresher look.

SITE CONDITIONS: Full sun to partial shade; moist, well-drained soils

HARDINESS: Zones 8A–11A

GARDEN TIPS: Hammock snakeroot makes a nice low shrub border, but also works well in naturalistic plantings and in mixed beds. Its blooms are especially delightful when paired with other flowering species.

WAYNE MATCHETT

SWAMP MILKWEED
(Asclepias incarnata, A. perennis)

1–6 ft.

Swamp milkweed—sometimes known as Pink milkweed and White milkweed—are striking wildflowers that make an excellent addition to moist, sunny landscapes. Both are great for attracting butterflies and other pollinating insects. Milkweed is the larval host plant for Monarch, Queen, and Soldier butterflies. It also is an important nectar source for these and other butterflies, including Pipevine, Spicebush, and Eastern swallowtails. Native sweat bees, leafcutter bees, and yellow-faced bees forage the flowers for pollen and nectar.

Asclepias flowers consist of petals that reflex backward and an upright crown (corona) of crested hoods that are often mistaken for petals. *A. incarnata* (pictured, top) flowers range in color from light pink to rose. Its leaves are lance- to linear-shaped and up to 6 inches long. *A. perennis* (pictured, bottom) produces white to pale pink flowers. It is a shorter, more delicate species of milkweed with smaller flowerheads and lance-shaped leaves. In both species, the small, flat seeds are born in follicles that split to release seeds. Attached to each seed is a silky white pappus that catches the wind and aids in dispersal.

FAMILY: Apocynaceae (dogbane family)

NATIVE RANGE: *A. incarnata* occurs in Central and South Florida; *A. perennis* is native to Central and North Florida.

LIFESPAN: Perennial

BLOOM SEASON: Summer and fall (*A. incarnata*); spring through fall (*A. perennis*)

GROWTH HABIT: 4–6' tall but not as wide (*A. incarnata*); 1–2' tall and almost as wide (*A. perennis*)

PROPAGATION: Collect seeds from plants once follicles split. Germinate on top of soil with a light mix barely covering seeds. Seeds can be stored in the refrigerator for a couple of months.

PLANTING: Plants are typically available in 4-inch, 6-inch, and 1-gallon containers. Space 2 to 3 feet apart in clusters of three or more plants.

CARE: Light annual pruning may be necessary to remove dead stems. Aphids frequently attack milkweeds; remove them manually to avoid pesticide use.

SITE CONDITIONS: *A. incarnata* does best in full sun but may adjust to partial shade. *A. perennis* can tolerate more shade. Both require moist to wet, well-drained soils.

HARDINESS: *A. incarnata* is suited for zones 8A–10B; *A. perennis* does best in zones 8A–9B.

GARDEN TIPS: Swamp milkweed works best in mixed butterfly and wildflower gardens planted along pond edges or similar moist sites. They can tolerate short periods of drought once established, but soil should be kept moist. Both species do well in containers.

CAUTION: Do not confuse this plant with the nonnative Tropical milkweed (*Asclepias curassavica*), which is typically sold at retail garden centers. Tropical milkweed does not die back in winter in Florida (as do native milkweeds) and can encourage overwintering in adult Monarchs. It also is linked to the transmission of the *Ophryocystis elektroscirrha* (OE) infection.

BUTTERFLYWEED
(Asclepias tuberosa)

1–3 ft.

Butterflyweed is a perennial wildflower that occurs naturally in sandhills, pine flatwoods, and other sandy uplands. It is the larval host of Monarch, Queen, and Soldier butterflies, and its blooms attract hummingbirds, bees, and other pollinators.

Butterflyweed's bright orange to reddish flowers are born in showy terminal umbels. Each flower has a reflexed corolla and an upright corona—a characteristic typical of milkweed flowers. Stems are rough to hairy. Leaves are coarse, narrowly ovate to lanceolate, and oppositely arranged. Seeds are born in erect follicles that dry and split open as the fruit matures. Each seed is attached to a white silky pappus that catches the wind and aids in dispersal.

Florida has two subspecies: *A. tuberosa* ssp. *rolfsii* is less bushy, has wavy leaf margins, and occurs throughout Florida. *A. tuberosa* ssp. *tuberosa* has flatter, narrow leaves and is often found in woodlands in northern Florida.

Asclepias tuberosa is an exception to the *Asclepias* genus in that its stem does not contain the milky latex that distinguishes the rest of the genus and gives it the common name "milkweed."

FAMILY: Apocynaceae (dogbane family)

NATIVE RANGE: Nearly throughout Florida

LIFESPAN: Perennial

BLOOM SEASON: Spring through fall

GROWTH HABIT: 1–3' tall with 1–2' spread

PROPAGATION: Cuttings, division, seed. Seeds can be stored in the refrigerator for a couple of months. Germinate on top of soil and cover lightly. Once sprouted, seedlings should be potted and allowed to grow to 3 inches before transplanting.

PLANTING: Plants are typically available in 6-inch and 1-gallon containers. Space them 2 feet apart in clusters of three or more, or mix with other bunchgrasses and wildflowers.

CARE: Most milkweeds require light annual pruning to remove dead stems.

SITE CONDITIONS: Full sun; dry, well-drained sandy soils

HARDINESS: Zones 8A–10B

GARDEN TIPS: Butterfly milkweed is an excellent addition to butterfly gardens as well as any dry, hot landscape. The Florida subspecies tends to be less bushy than its northern counterpart.

CAUTION: Do not confuse this plant with the nonnative Tropical milkweed (*Asclepias curassavica*), which is typically sold at big box retail garden centers. Tropical milkweed does not die back in winter in Florida (as do native milkweeds) and can encourage overwintering in adult Monarchs. It is also linked to the transmission of the *Ophryocystis elektroscirrha* (OE) infection.

HERB-OF-GRACE
(Bacopa monnieri)

1–3 in.

Also known as Water hyssop, Herb-of-grace is a creeping, mat-forming perennial that occurs naturally in coastal hammocks and swales, swamps, salt and freshwater marshes, and along river, stream, and ditch edges. It attracts a variety of small pollinators and is a larval host plant for the White peacock butterfly.

The pinkish-white flowers are bell-shaped and five-lobed with a violet center. Each has four stamens and five sepals. Flowers are axillary with small stalks. The bloom's center is violet. Leaves are sessile, obovate to spatulate, and succulent. They are oppositely arranged. Leaf margins are entire. Stems are succulent and bright green. Fruits are inconspicuous capsules.

Herb-of-grace is similar in appearance to its cousin, Lemon bacopa (*Bacopa caroliniana*), and is found in similar habitats. To differentiate them, crush a leaf. If you smell lemon, you know you have Lemon bacopa. Herb-of-grace will not emit a scent. Other distinguishing factors are Lemon bacopa's purplish-blue flowers and clasping leaves.

The species epithet *monniere* pays homage to Louis-Guillaume Le Monnier (1717–1799), a French natural scientist.

FAMILY: Plantaginaceae (plantain family)

NATIVE RANGE: Nearly throughout Florida

LIFESPAN: Perennial

BLOOM SEASON: Spring through fall, but may bloom year-round

GROWTH HABIT: 1–3" tall and sprawling

PROPAGATION: Plants can be divided or runners lifted and placed on soil to root.

PLANTING: Plants are available as bare root and in 1-gallon containers. Space 12 to 36 inches apart, depending on how quickly cover is desired. Place where rainwater drains but does not stand for long periods.

CARE: No special care is needed.

SITE CONDITIONS: Full sun; moist to wet sandy soils

HARDINESS: Zones 8B–11A

GARDEN TIPS: In the right conditions, Herb-of-grace can make a nice groundcover. It also works well in a container, hanging pot, or aquarium. It does not tolerate long periods of drought. Herb-of-grace will generally die back in winter, although in southern Florida it can be evergreen.

FLORIDA GREENEYES
(Berlandiera subacaulis)

1–1½ ft.

Florida greeneyes is a perennial herbaceous wildflower endemic to Florida. It occurs naturally in sandhills, dry pine flatwoods, and mixed upland forests, as well as along dry roadsides. Its bright blooms attract a variety of bees and butterflies.

Florida greeneyes' flowers consist of vibrant yellow ray florets surrounding a head of greenish-yellow tubular disk florets. The flowers are held at their base by a cup of bright green bracts. The plant's dark green basal leaves are ovately shaped with crenate margins when young; as they mature, they become more deeply lobed. Its stem is hairy. The taproot is thick and tuberous. Seeds develop in bracts and mature into a distinctive, platelike seedhead. Only ray florets produce seed.

The genus name *Berlandiera* is named for the 19th-century French botanist Jean-Louis Berlandier, who collected botanicals in Mexico and Texas. The species epithet *subacaulis* is from the Latin *sub*, meaning "under," and *acaule*, or "stemless." It refers to the plant's short stem.

FAMILY: Asteraceae (aster, composite, or daisy family)

NATIVE RANGE: Eastern Panhandle, north and central peninsula, Lee and Monroe counties

LIFESPAN: Perennial

BLOOM SEASON: Spring and summer in the north, but may bloom year-round in southern Florida

GROWTH HABIT: 1–1½' tall when blooming

PROPAGATION: Seeds can be collected after ray florets drop. Propagation by division is possible but may be difficult, as plants are joined by a thick tuberous root.

PLANTING: Space plants as close as 12 inches apart or mix with grasses and other wildflowers.

CARE: Cut old flowerheads to extend flowering and help keep the plant looking neat.

SITE CONDITIONS: Full sun to minimal shade; dry, well-drained sandy or rocky soils

HARDINESS: Zones 8B–10B

GARDEN TIPS: Florida greeneyes is easy to establish in the garden. Its tuberous root, which can be as thick as 12 inches in older plants, makes it very drought tolerant. Once established, Florida greeneyes can form large clumps and produce copious blooms, creating a beautiful display.

MARY KEIM

BUSHY SEASIDE OXEYE
(Borrichia frutescens)

2–4 ft.

Bushy seaside oxeye is a perennial shrub with attractive daisy-like blooms. It is known by many common names, including Sea-oxeye daisy, Sea marigold, Beach carnation, Seaside tansy, and Silver sea-oxeye. It occurs naturally in coastal strands, mangroves, beach dunes, salt marshes, and tidal flats. The flowers are attractive to a variety of pollinators, including Gulf fritillary, Southern white, and Orange sulphur butterflies. The seeds provide food for birds and other small wildlife.

Each flower is composed of 15 to 30 yellow ray florets surrounding many stiff yellow-orange disk florets with conspicuous black anthers. Flowers are approximately 1 inch in diameter. Leaves are oval to lanceolate, grayish green, and pubescent, giving the foliage a silvery sheen. Margins are entire but may be toothed toward the base. Fruit is a dark-colored achene containing a single seed.

The genus name *Borrichia* is named for the Danish scientist Ole Borch (1626–1690). The species epithet *frutescens* is Latin for "to become bushy" and refers to the plant's shrublike growth habit.

FAMILY: Asteraceae (aster, composite, or daisy family)

NATIVE RANGE: All peninsular coastal counties from Duval to Taylor, as well as Wakulla, Franklin, Bay, and Santa Rosa

LIFESPAN: Perennial

BLOOM SEASON: Year-round, with peak blooming in spring and summer

GROWTH HABIT: 2–4' tall

PROPAGATION: Break up dry seedheads and scatter. Top with light soil and keep moist. Plants can be carefully divided.

PLANTING: Plants are available in 3- and 4-gallon containers. Plan for plants to spread over time.

CARE: Deadheading or cutting back flowerheads may increase blooming.

SITE CONDITIONS: Full sun to minimal shade; moist to wet soils (plants can tolerate occasionally inundated soils)

HARDINESS: Zones 8B–11A

GARDEN TIPS: Bushy seaside oxeye is highly salt tolerant. It can tolerate drought for short periods and can withstand occasional saltwater inundation. It is excellent for coastal restorations and landscapes. It works well as a border planting, in a mixed wildflower garden, and along retention pond edges. The plant is rhizomatous and can form colonies that may persist for many years.

ALAN CRESSLER

YELLOW CANNA
(Canna flaccida)

3–4 ft.

Also known as Golden canna or Bandanna-of-the-Everglades, Yellow canna is a robust aquatic wildflower with large, showy, orchid-like blooms. It occurs naturally in freshwater marshes and swamps and along pond and lake margins throughout much of Florida. It is the larval host for the Brazilian (or Canna) skipper, which will roll the leaf into a tube around its body as a means of protection from predators and extreme sun exposure. Dragonfly larvae have also been known to hide in the leaves until they change into adults. Bees and butterflies are attracted to the flower's nectar.

Yellow canna flowers are composed of three bright yellow petals and three greenish-yellow sepals that are fused at the base, forming a tubelike structure. Petal lips are broad and drooping. Each flower is subtended by a single bract. Flowers are born in terminal clusters. They are short-lived, opening in late evening and closing by midday. Leaves are long, smooth, and broadly lanceolate with entire margins and pointed tips. They are alternately arranged and spiral around the smooth, fleshy stem. Fruits are long (2 to 3 inches) capsules with rough surfaces. They contain many small, black pellet-like seeds.

About 20 species of *Canna* are known from the Americas, but *Canna flaccida* is the only species that can grow in partially inundated conditions.

FAMILY: Cannaceae (canna family)

NATIVE RANGE: Peninsular Florida, a few Panhandle counties

LIFESPAN: Perennial

BLOOM SEASON: Spring through early fall

GROWTH HABIT: 3–4' tall

PROPAGATION: Division, seed (must be scarified)

PLANTING: Bare root, liner, 1-gallon and 3-gallon containers are generally available. Space plants 18 to 36 inches apart; they will fill in quite rapidly. Place where water inundation will not exceed 12 inches during the wet season.

CARE: Occasional removal of old stems and seed pods may be necessary to maintain a neat appearance. Removal of excess plants will help keep them from dominating a wet area. Enjoy the leaf rollers and watch them mature.

SITE CONDITIONS: Full sun to partial shade; moist to inundated sandy, loamy, or clay soils

HARDINESS: Zones 8A–11A

GARDEN TIPS: Yellow canna has a robust tuberous rhizome that helps the plant survive tough conditions such as drought or freezing temperatures. The plant tends to spread quickly by suckering. It can be used in rain gardens; along pond and lake edges; in ditches, swales, and marshes; and for naturalistic or restoration wetlands.

JOSHUA DOBY

FLORIDA PAINTBRUSH
(Carphephorus corymbosus)

Also known as a Coastalplain chaffhead, Florida paintbrush is a showy herbaceous wildflower that blooms from late summer into fall. It occurs naturally in pine, scrubby, and dry to mesic flatwoods; sandhills; and ruderal areas. Its large,

2–3 ft.

striking flower clusters are very attractive to butterflies and other pollinators.

Flowers are born in large flat-topped corymbs. Each bloom is composed of many bright pink to lavender tubular disk florets and no ray florets. The inflorescence appears atop an erect, unbranched stem that emerges from a basal rosette. Basal leaves are flat, linear, and succulent in appearance; stem leaves are sessile and alternately arranged. Stems are covered in tiny hairs. The fruit is an achene-like cypsela with a rough surface and a tuft of bristly hairs.

The species epithet *corymbosus* is from the Latin *corymbus*, meaning "cluster of fruit or flowers."

FAMILY: Asteraceae (aster, composite, or daisy family)

NATIVE RANGE: Peninsular Florida, Bay and Jackson counties

LIFESPAN: Perennial

BLOOM SEASON: Summer and fall

GROWTH HABIT: 2–3' tall when blooming

PROPAGATION: Seed

PLANTING: Plants are available in quart and 1-gallon containers. This striking wildflower can be planted in small groups 12 to 16 inches apart and mixed with other wildflowers or bunchgrasses.

CARE: Spent flowerheads can be left until spring for added color interest or cut to collect seed.

SITE CONDITIONS: Full sun to minimal shade; dry, well-drained sandy soils

HARDINESS: Zones 8A–10B

GARDEN TIPS: Florida paintbrush is a star for attracting butterflies and makes a great addition to formal and naturalistic landscapes. It is easy to integrate and maintain.

OTHER SPECIES: Vanillaleaf (*C. odoratissimus*) occurs naturally in mesic to hydric pine flatwoods from North Florida to northern Central Florida. As leaves dry, they emit a vanilla scent when crushed. Vanillaleaf was formerly collected from the wild to flavor tobacco, but was found to be carcinogenic when smoked. Pineland purple (*C. subtropicanus*) is found in dry to mesic flatwoods from southern Central Florida through South Florida, except the Keys. The plant has no vanilla scent. Although the two species differ slightly in form, they both bloom from late summer into fall with panicles of deep lavender florets.

PARTRIDGE PEA
(Chamaecrista fasciculata)

3 ft.

Partridge pea is an herbaceous annual or short-lived perennial that occurs naturally in scrub, sandhills, flatwoods, beach dunes, and disturbed areas throughout the state. Flowers appear from late spring through late fall except in South Florida, where they are year-round. The blooms attract mostly butterflies and long-tongued bees, while ants, flies, wasps, and other bees are attracted to nectar glands that grow on leaf stems. Seeds are consumed by birds and other wildlife. Partridge pea is a host plant for several species of butterflies, including the Gray hairstreak and Cloudless sulphur. Despite its appeal to so many insects, the flower is pollinated only by long-tongued bees.

The axillary flowers are yellow with reddish spots at the base of each petal. They bear both yellow and reddish-purple anthers; the latter contains reproductive pollen, while the former produces food pollen. Leaves are pinnately compound with many small yellow-green leaflets that fold up when touched. Nectar is produced at the base of the leaf in tiny, reddish-orange glands. Stems and branches are typically dark red. Seeds are born in narrow, flattened pods.

FAMILY: Fabaceae (legume, bean, or pea family)

NATIVE RANGE: Nearly throughout Florida

LIFESPAN: Annual

BLOOM SEASON: Late spring through late fall

GROWTH HABIT: Variable, up to 3' tall with 2–3' spread

PROPAGATION: Collect seed pods in the fall once they have turned brown and are falling from the plant. Seeds will germinate where they fall, or scatter them in new areas and cover lightly.

PLANTING: Quart- and gallon-container plants are available. Plant about 2 feet apart.

CARE: Many seedlings may germinate in rainy years and may require some removal.

SITE CONDITIONS: Full sun to partial shade; very dry, well-drained sandy to loamy soils

HARDINESS: Zones 8A–10B

GARDEN TIPS: Partridge pea is an excellent plant to use in disturbed areas, as it tends to establish quickly. It is a prolific self-seeder and also is fairly salt tolerant. Partridge pea is a nitrogen fixer, so it may improve and enrich soils, allowing for the introduction of more demanding plants into your landscape.

MARYLAND GOLDENASTER
(Chrysopsis mariana)

18 in.

Florida has 11 native goldenaster species, 8 of which are endemic; several are listed by the state as rare or endangered. Maryland goldenaster (*Chrysopsis mariana*) is found in pinelands, sandhills, and sandy roadsides. Native butterflies as well as a variety of native long-tongued bees—including green metallic, sweat, leafcutter, bumble, and mining bees—are attracted to the plant's nectar.

Maryland goldenaster's yellow daisy-like flowers are born in terminal clusters. The loosely hairy but bright green stem leaves are broadest at the tip and alternately arranged. Fruit is an achene. Plants are compact with many stems.

The genus name *Chrysopsis* is from the Greek *khrusós*, or "gold," and *ópsis*, or "resembling in appearance." It refers to the plant's gold-colored flowers.

FAMILY: Asteraceae (aster, composite, or daisy family)

NATIVE RANGE: Throughout Florida, except the extreme south

LIFESPAN: Perennial

BLOOM SEASON: Spring through fall

GROWTH HABIT: 18" tall when flowering

PROPAGATION: Sow seed in well-drained soil in late fall or winter.

PLANTING: Plants are available in 1-gallon containers and can be planted any time. Space 18 to 24 inches apart. Because the species is widespread north of Florida, make sure plants are grown from a local source.

CARE: Resist the temptation to nip back goldenaster's stems; doing so will reduce its ability to flower. When stems die and become brittle, they may be trimmed from the plant.

SITE CONDITIONS: Full sun to minimal (high pine) shade; dry to moist, well-drained sandy soils

HARDINESS: Zones 8A–9B

GARDEN TIPS: Use Maryland goldenaster in mixed wildflower and bunchgrass settings or in small masses that will attract the eye when in bloom. Its compact shape and tips covered with blooms make it a desirable landscape plant.

OTHER SPECIES: Coastalplain goldenaster (*Chrysopsis scabrella*) is a biennial species with shaggy-haired foliage and leggy growth. It occurs in the dry sandy soils of sandhills and scrub and attracts abundant pollinators. The densely hairy, silvery foliage of Florida goldenaster (*Chrysopsis floridana*), an endangered species found in scrub habitat in only five Central Florida counties, makes it a show-stopper. Both species are easy to grow and worthy of a garden setting.

MISTFLOWER
(Conoclinium coelestinum)

1–3 ft.

Mistflower, Blue mistflower, Wild ageratum, Pink eupatorium, Hardy ageratum, and Blue boneset are just some of the many common names used to identify this eye-catching Florida native wildflower. Found in riverine swamps, moist meadows, and roadside ditches, its flowers give the appearance of a blue fog when blooming en masse. Flowers are very attractive to pollinators, especially butterflies, moths, and long-tongued bees.

Mistflower's many branched stems bear dense, flat clusters of disk florets that vary in color from bright blue to lavender to pinkish white. Ray florets are absent. Long protruding stamens give the flowerheads a fuzzy appearance. Light green linear bracts surround the flower base. Leaves are almost triangular in shape, with toothed margins and faintly pubescent surfaces. They are petiolate and oppositely arranged. Fruits are small achenes with tiny hairs that aid in wind distribution. Roots are rhizomatous.

The species epithet *coelestinum* is from the Latin *caelestis* (*coelestis*), meaning "celestial" or "heavenly." It refers to the sky-blue color of the flowers.

FAMILY: Asteraceae (aster, composite, or daisy family)

NATIVE RANGE: Throughout Florida

LIFESPAN: Perennial

BLOOM SEASON: Spring through fall

GROWTH HABIT: 1–3' tall

PROPAGATION: Division, seed

PLANTING: Available in 1-gallon containers. Plant 2 to 3 feet apart to allow for spread. Moist to wet soils are best; dryer soils may require less sun or extra water.

CARE: Cut back in late winter to encourage new growth.

SITE CONDITIONS: Full sun to partial shade; moist to wet sandy, loamy, or mucky soils

HARDINESS: Zones 8A–11A

GARDEN TIPS: Mistflower is perfect for a wildflower garden where it can naturalize freely, particularly in a moist, partially shaded setting.

CAUTION: Mistflower has a wide range throughout the East and Midwest. Many cultivars have been developed, so be sure to buy locally sourced plants. *Praxelis clematidea* is a very aggressive invader that looks a lot like Mistflower. The flowerheads are taller than wide, its seeds are black, and its leaves smell like cat urine when crushed. It grows in drier soils and is usually found in disturbed sites.

ELEANOR DIETRICH

FALSE ROSEMARY
(Conradina canescens, C. grandiflora)

False rosemary (*Conradina*) is a genus of evergreen shrubs that rewards gardeners with a spring display of fragrant blooms. It is attractive to some butterflies and moths but mostly attracts native bees, including large carpenter and digger bees. Two species are commonly available: *C. canescens* occurs in scrub and dune habitats in the western Panhandle; *C. grandiflora* (pictured) occurs in coastal counties in the central and southern peninsula on scrubby sites.

Conradina flowers are purplish white and two-lipped; the lower lip is three-lobed and bears dark purple spots. Stamens are prominent and run along the inside of the upper lip. *C. grandiflora*'s flowers are larger and more upright than *C. canescens*. Sepals are fused and finely pubescent. Leaves are short and needlelike with a silvery-green hue. They grow densely from upright stems that branch from a main woody stem.

False rosemary plants may look like their namesake cousin, whose leaves are used as a savory cooking spice, but these members of the mint family emit a minty-fresh smell when their leaves are crushed.

2–3 ft.

FAMILY: Lamiaceae (mint family)

NATIVE RANGE: *C. canescens* occurs in the western Panhandle; *C. grandiflora* is found in coastal counties in the central and southern peninsula.

LIFESPAN: Perennial

BLOOM SEASON: Spring through fall, with peak bloom in early spring

GROWTH HABIT: 2–3' tall and wide

PROPAGATION: Cuttings, seed. To propagate from seed, harvest when fresh and sow in spring in well-drained soil. Keep moist until germination occurs.

PLANTING: Plants are readily available in 1- and occasionally 3-gallon containers. Space plants 30 to 36 inches apart and water until established.

CARE: *Conradina* may be trimmed after flowering, but most gardeners leave it alone and enjoy its beautiful natural form. Sections of older, well-established plants may die suddenly; remove these to encourage new growth. Because this plant thrives naturally in dry ecosystems, overwatering may cause rot and decline.

SITE CONDITIONS: Full sun; dry, well-drained sandy soils

HARDINESS: *C. grandiflora* is suited for zones 9A–9B; *C. canescens* is best for 8A–9B.

GARDEN TIPS: This versatile ground-cover can be used in mass plantings, as a single specimen, or in a pot. Both are very drought resistant once established. *Conradina* thrives on natural rainfall. If your landscape is irrigated on a regular basis, look for a spot that remains dry.

CAUTION: Of the six *Conradina* species in the state, all but *C. canescens* are endangered or threatened and thus limited in population. Because these species can hybridize, it is important to plant the species found naturally in your area to help preserve the distinct genetic identities and ecological roles of these plants. Along the central and southern east coast, choose *C. grandiflora*. Ask your nursery supplier for the species native to your locale.

LEAVENWORTH'S TICKSEED
(Coreopsis leavenworthii)

1½–2½ ft.

Florida's state wildflower is *Coreopsis*, also known as tickseed, and refers to all 12 species native to Florida. Many of these occur only in North Florida and the Panhandle. The most common species, Leavenworth's tickseed (pictured, top), is almost entirely endemic to Florida, which means it occurs naturally nowhere else in the world. This plant can be found throughout Florida, especially on roadsides and in disturbed areas, flatwoods, and prairies. *Coreopsis* is a great nectar plant for butterflies and pollinators.

The 1- to 2-inch flowers have dark disk florets surrounded by scalloped yellow ray florets. Its bright green leaves are narrow and range from simple to lobed or deeply divided, thus giving the plant a more open appearance. Stems are slender and glabrous with many branches. Seeds are born in awned achenes with membranous wings.

FAMILY: Asteraceae (aster, composite, or daisy family)

NATIVE RANGE: Nearly throughout Florida

LIFESPAN: Annual (short-lived perennial in South Florida)

BLOOM SEASON: Year-round

GROWTH HABIT: 1½–2½' tall

PROPAGATION: Look for mature seeds with "wings" on their sides in the little cup at the tip of the stem after flower petals have withered. Germination usually occurs in less than seven days.

PLANTING: Leavenworth's tickseed is available in quarts and gallons. Space 1 to 2 feet apart. They may be planted any time of the year; plant in the spring for the full benefit of flowering. *Coreopsis* establishes quickly in moist soils.

CARE: This plant is relatively free of disease and pests, though some critters may feed on it. If the plants are cut back near the end of their bloom, they will produce another flush of flowers. Plants can be string-trimmed or mowed to 6 or 8 inches.

SITE CONDITIONS: Full sun; moist, well-drained sandy soils

HARDINESS: Zones 8A–11A

GARDEN TIPS: Leavenworth's tickseed needs a site that offers space for it to reseed. It can reseed between other plants, such as other wildflowers, if they are not too competitive. Though it can tolerate some drought and drier soils, it will not perform as well. Moist soils also allow for reseeding—important in maintaining this species.

OTHER SPECIES: Lanceleaf tickseed (*C. lanceolata*) (pictured, bottom) grows naturally in North Florida and the Panhandle in sandhills and disturbed areas, but it is widely used farther south. It is a short-lived perennial that readily reseeds. Its yellow ray flowers are complemented by a golden disk atop fairly thick stems. This spring bloomer can flower into summer with deadheading and is drought tolerant.

CAUTION: For *Coreopsis leavenworthii*, which occurs throughout Florida, the origin of the plants or seed does not seem to be a factor in successful growth, according to recent research. If other species of *Coreopsis* are being considered, look for local sources, as most other species also occur far outside of Florida. Some, such as Lanceleaf tickseed (*C. lanceolata*), also have popular horticultural varieties developed from progeny outside Florida.

OBLONGLEAF TWINFLOWER
(Dyschoriste oblongifolia)

6–10 in.

Oblongleaf twinflower is a low growing wildflower found in dry to moist sandhills, flatwoods, and mixed upland forests in North and Central Florida. It attracts bees and butterflies, including the Malachite and White peacock, and is a host plant for the Common buckeye. Look for small pale green eggs laid singly on leaves. Common buckeye caterpillars eat both leaves and flowers and may be seen on the plants year-round, especially in fall.

Oblongleaf twinflower has small (1-inch) blooms that are light blue to purple and funnel-shaped, with five lobed petals. The lower petals bear dark marks or streaks that extend into the throat. Each bloom has four stamens and five lobed calyces that are pubescent and subtend the flower. Leaves are simple, oblong, dark green, and pubescent. They are oppositely arranged on thin stems. Fruits are capsules that, when mature, dry and split open, dispersing the seeds.

The common name "twinflower" refers to its flowers being born in pairs along the stems.

FAMILY: Acanthaceae (acanthus family)

NATIVE RANGE: Central and eastern Panhandle, north and central peninsula

LIFESPAN: Perennial

BLOOM SEASON: Spring through fall; year-round in the south

GROWTH HABIT: 6–10" and spreading

PROPAGATION: Cuttings, division, seed. Take stem cuttings or divide clumps in summer.

PLANTING: Plants are available in 1-gallon containers. Space plants 18 to 24 inches apart.

CARE: In winter, plants are semi-dormant and can be trimmed or mown to 3 inches to freshen. Plants will go dormant in areas that receive frost but will quickly recover in spring.

SITE CONDITIONS: Full sun to partial shade; dry to moist, acidic, well-drained sandy soils

HARDINESS: Zones 8A–11A

GARDEN TIPS: Oblongleaf twinflower is exceptionally adaptable to the home garden. It has an extended bloom period and will spread rapidly by underground runners and self-sown seed, making it an excellent, easy-to-care-for groundcover. Planting in partial shade will result in less dense coverage. Although drought tolerant, extended dry periods may harm the plant; it will be necessary to water occasionally. Twinflower is not salt tolerant, making it a poor candidate for coastal landscapes.

BUTTON RATTLESNAKEMASTER
(Eryngium yuccifolium)

3 ft.

Button rattlesnakemaster is a peculiar perennial wildflower that occurs in moist pinelands and savannas throughout Florida. Its flowers bloom late spring through fall. They are frequented by a variety of pollinators but are of special value to native bees. The plant is a larval host for the Black swallowtail butterfly and attracts many predatory and parasitoid insects that prey on garden pests. It also attracts bats.

Eryngium species lack the characteristic umbellate flower form of their Apiaceae family cousins. Rather, the umbel is compacted into a tight, prominently globose flowerhead, reminiscent of an aster. In *E. yuccifolium*, the flowerhead may be up to 1 inch in diameter and is composed of many tiny whitish-green flowers. It is subtended by silvery bracts and born on erect, multibranched stems. Leaves are long (2 to 3 feet), linear or grasslike, and taper to a point. They have a succulent appearance and grow in stemless rosettes. Stem leaves are smaller, stiff, and alternately arranged. Leaf venation is parallel. Leaf margins are armed with evenly spaced spines. Fruit is a schizocarp that splits into a pair of inconspicuous carpels at maturity.

FAMILY: Apiaceae (Umbelliferae) (carrot, celery, or parsley family)

NATIVE RANGE: Nearly throughout Florida

LIFESPAN: Perennial

BLOOM SEASON: Spring through fall

GROWTH HABIT: 3'± tall and 1–3' wide

PROPAGATION: Germinate seed on moist soil and cover slightly.

PLANTING: Plants are available in quart to 3-gallon containers. Space 12 to 18 inches apart.

CARE: Old flower stalks may be trimmed at the end of the season.

SITE CONDITIONS: Full sun to partial shade; moist to wet or inundated sandy, loamy, or calcareous soils

HARDINESS: Zones 8A–10A

GARDEN TIPS: Button rattlesnakemaster is a good choice for difficult areas because it is adaptable to a variety of soil and moisture conditions. It does well in low-nutrient or fertile soils but is not salt tolerant. Its unique growth habit, interesting flower form, and attractive foliage make it a nice addition to wildflower gardens and naturalistic landscapes.

CAUTION: Button rattlesnakemaster has several known cultivars. Be sure to purchase from local growers.

PINELAND HELIOTROPE
(Euploca polyphylla)

6–12 in.

Pineland heliotrope is an herbaceous wildflower endemic to Florida. It occurs naturally in pine rocklands, wet prairies, coastal thickets, and ruderal areas. It typically blooms throughout the year, but in North Florida it may bloom only in fall. It produces copious amounts of flowers, attracting a variety of pollinators, especially small butterflies.

Pineland heliotrope's many small flowers may be yellow or white and are born on distinctly curved spikes. The yellow-flowered form tends to be erect and upright, while the white-flowered form has a more prostrate and creeping habit. Though the two forms are quite distinct in growth habit, they are considered one species with no varietal status. Stems are pubescent. Leaves are narrowly elliptic to 1 inch long and sessile with a smooth upper surface and densely pubescent underside. They are alternately arranged. The fruit is a small schizocarp containing up to four nutlets.

This plant was recently reclassified as *Euploca polyphylla*, although many sources still refer to its original name, *Heliotropium polyphyllum*. The common name "heliotrope" comes from the Greek *hélios*, or "sun," and *trepein*, or "to turn." It refers to the belief that the plants turn their flowers toward the sun.

FAMILY: Boraginaceae (borage or forget-me-not family)

NATIVE RANGE: Peninsula south into the Keys, Escambia County

LIFESPAN: Perennial

BLOOM SEASON: Year-round

GROWTH HABIT: 6–12"+ tall (1–3" for prostrate form) and much wider

PROPAGATION: Cuttings, seeds (may be difficult to germinate)

PLANTING: Plants can be purchased in 1-gallon containers. Plant as a ground-cover about 2 feet apart where it can spread without much effort to control. It can also be planted with other wildflowers in a mixed garden.

CARE: This plant may continue to send out new roots as it spreads across the landscape. This can be a welcome feature but may require frequent pruning to keep in check. Cold temperatures may knock the foliage back; allow it to begin to regrow before pruning.

SITE CONDITIONS: Full sun to minimal shade; moderately dry to moist, well-drained sandy or calcareous soils

HARDINESS: Zones 8A–11A

GARDEN TIPS: Pineland heliotrope is adaptable to many growing conditions, making it an excellent addition to butterfly and wildflower gardens as well as in the home landscape. It suckers and can form large patches, making it a great low groundcover. It is drought tolerant and can grow in nutrient-poor soils but is not particularly salt tolerant.

NARROWLEAF YELLOWTOPS
(Flaveria linearis)

2–3 ft.

Narrowleaf yellowtops occurs naturally in depression and basin marshes, wet prairies, pine rocklands, hydric hammocks, mangrove swamp and tidal marsh edges, and sand dunes, as well as in disturbed or ruderal areas. Many butterflies nectar on its flowers, which also attract bees and flower beetles.

Narrowleaf yellowtops' inflorescence is a showy corymb of bright yellow flowers that are somewhat flat-topped (hence the common name). Individual flowers are composed of several disk florets and a single ray floret. They are small but great in number. Leaves are linear, sessile, and oppositely arranged. Leaf margins are typically entire but may be somewhat toothed. Branched stems are glabrous and may be reddish in color. Seeds are born in achenes.

The genus name *Flaveria* is from the Latin *flavens* (*flaveo*), meaning "gold" or "yellow" and alludes to the flower color. The species epithet *linearis* is Latin for "consisting of lines" or "linear," referring to the leaf shape.

FAMILY: Asteraceae (aster, composite, or daisy family)

NATIVE RANGE: Most coastal peninsular counties from Levy and St. Johns south to the Keys; Taylor, Wakulla, Jefferson, and Madison counties in the Panhandle

LIFESPAN: Perennial

BLOOM SEASON: Spring through fall

GROWTH HABIT: 2–3' tall; usually wider than tall

PROPAGATION: Cuttings root easily in damp soil. Plants reseed readily.

PLANTING: Plants are available in 1-gallon containers. Space plants 2 to 3 feet apart for masses, or mix with other wildflowers where its size will not overwhelm other plants.

CARE: The plant can appear ratty after flowering, so pruning may be desired. Cut back in spring for fresh growth. Wear gloves, as the sap may irritate skin. Overwatering or rich soils will result in taller, lankier plants.

SITE CONDITIONS: Full sun to minimal shade; moist to seasonally inundated, well-drained, nutrient-poor sandy or mucky soils

HARDINESS: Zones 8A–11A

GARDEN TIPS: Narrowleaf yellowtops is a tough plant that has a high tolerance for stress. It does well in urban settings and areas where soil may be disturbed. It is highly drought, pest, and salt tolerant (but not in frontline dunes). Because it grows low and wide, it does well in mixed plantings and as a tall groundcover.

BLANKETFLOWER
(Gaillardia pulchella)

12–18 in.

Also known as Indian blanket and Firewheel, Blanketflower occurs throughout Florida in coastal dunes, dry savannahs, and other dry, open, or disturbed sites. Its colorful blooms attract a variety of pollinating insects.

Blanketflower's ray florets typically are bicolored with an inner red band surrounded by an outer yellow band. However, flowers also can be entirely red or yellow, have an inner red band surrounded by a white band, or, on rare occasions, be entirely white. Rarely, flowers may be tubular—narrow at the base and flaring out like trumpets. The flower's center disk florets are dark red to purplish. Leaves are linear- to lance-shaped and quite hairy, which makes the plant appear grayish green.

FAMILY: Asteraceae (aster, composite, or daisy family)

NATIVE RANGE: Scattered throughout Florida in 27 counties but favoring the east coast

LIFESPAN: Annual or short-lived perennial

BLOOM SEASON: Mid-spring to late summer; year-round in Central and South Florida

GROWTH HABIT: 12–18" tall; can easily spread to twice that

PROPAGATION: Sow seed where desired and cover lightly.

PLANTING: Plants are available in 4-inch, quart, and gallon containers. For a dense bed, space plants about 12 to 18 inches apart.

CARE: Established plants are drought tolerant, but supplemental watering might be needed during extended dry periods. Deadheading of spent flowerheads and occasional removal of older plants is recommended. No cold protection is

needed during winter; even the tiniest seedlings tolerate frost and freezes into the low 20s.

SITE CONDITIONS: Full sun; dry to slightly dry, well-drained sandy soils

HARDINESS: Zones 8A–11A

GARDEN TIPS: Blanketflower's brightly colored flowers, long blooming season, and drought tolerance make this a popular garden plant. It is relatively pest and disease free, and does well in difficult conditions such as in coastal landscapes, roadsides, and parking lots. Use it where it can be allowed to spread, as it can be a very aggressive re-seeder.

CAUTION: Varieties sold at many large retail outlets and garden centers, and by national wildflower seed companies, are usually nonnative *Gaillardia aristata* or varieties of *G. pulchella* or *Gaillardia* × *grandiflora* (a hybrid of *G. pulchella* and *G. aristata*). Avoid planting these in the vicinity of Florida native ecotype *G. pulchella*, as they may hybridize.

BEACH VERBENA
(Glandularia maritima)

8–12 in.

Also known as Coastal mock vervain, Beach verbena is a short-lived perennial wildflower endemic primarily to Florida's east coast. This state-listed endangered species blooms year-round, although the most prolific flowering occurs in spring and summer. Beach verbena flowers are a good nectar source for a variety of butterflies and moths, including Gulf fritillaries, hawkmoths, and Long-tailed skippers. They also are attractive to miner bees and long-tongued bees, such as bumble and orchid bees.

Beach verbena's deep pink to lavender flowers are five-lobed and born in flat-topped terminal clusters. Leaves are dark green, glossy, and ovate to rhombic with deeply toothed or lobed margins. They are oppositely arranged. Stems have tiny hairs and are angled and generally prostrate. They will drop roots as they spread. Seeds are born in an inconspicuous nutlet.

FAMILY: Verbenaceae (verbena family)

NATIVE RANGE: East coast of peninsula from St. Johns to Monroe counties; Collier, Hendry, and Levy counties

LIFESPAN: Perennial

BLOOM SEASON: Year-round, with peak bloom in spring and summer

GROWTH HABIT: 8–12" tall with 2'+ spread

PROPAGATION: Cuttings, division, seed

PLANTING: Plants should be spaced from 3 to 4 feet apart to allow for their spread.

CARE: Light pruning may be necessary in more formal settings; otherwise, plants are relatively maintenance free. Do not over-irrigate.

SITE CONDITIONS: Full sun; dry, well-drained, acidic or alkaline clay, loamy, or sandy soils that are nutrient poor

HARDINESS: Zones 8B–11A

GARDEN TIPS: Use Beach verbena as a low groundcover in a sunny bed or woodland edge, or in a container or aboveground planter. It is particularly striking when used in masses. When planting, allow enough space for the plants to spread. Try Beach verbena in dry, low-nutrient soils where other plants have trouble growing. The plant is highly adaptable and is tolerant of drought and salty winds.

CAUTION: There are many nonnative verbenas available. Be sure to ask your nursery or supplier for native species. Verbena species may hybridize, so it is important to plant the species found naturally in your area to help preserve the distinct genetic identities and ecological roles of these plants.

ANDREA ENGLAND

NARROWLEAF SUNFLOWER
(Helianthus angustifolius)

4–6 ft.

Narrowleaf sunflower (also known as Swamp sunflower) is one of Florida's most common sunflowers. It occurs naturally in marshes, wet flatwoods, and roadside ditches throughout North and Central Florida. It blooms primarily in October and November, although some flowering can occur in September and December. In nature, it tends to form dense colonies, resulting in spectacular swaths of sunshine yellow. Narrowleaf sunflower blooms attract bees and butterflies, while its seeds provide a tasty treat for birds.

Narrowleaf sunflower's showy golden flowers are up to 3 inches across, with bright yellow, strap-shaped ray florets surrounding a compact head of reddish-brown disk florets. Flowerheads are cupped in green hairy bracts. Leaves are long, linear to acicular, and have a rough, sandpaper-like surface. Leaf margins are entire or may be revolute. Leaf arrangement is alternate toward the top of the stem and opposite below. Stems are rough and branched.

FAMILY: Asteraceae (aster, composite, or daisy family)

NATIVE RANGE: Panhandle, North and Central Florida south to Lake Okeechobee

LIFESPAN: Perennial

BLOOM SEASON: Late summer and fall

GROWTH HABIT: 4–6' tall

PROPAGATION: Division, seed

PLANTING: Plants are available in 1- and 3-gallon containers. Space plants 2 to 3 feet apart. Plants will spread via rhizomes to form masses, so place where that is a useful feature.

CARE: At the end of the bloom season (or once the seeds have provided treats for birds), the plants can be cut back to the ground. Stems also can be pinched back in late spring or early summer to encourage shorter, bushier growth and more blooms.

SITE CONDITIONS: Full sun; moist, acidic soils

HARDINESS: Zones 8A–10A

GARDEN TIPS: Narrowleaf sunflower is most suitable for large, open, wet sites such as a buffer along wetlands, or planted in a sunny moist meadow; along a lake edge, retention pond, or ditch; or in the back of a bog garden. Because of its height and its propensity to form large clusters, it is not recommended for small gardens or formal landscapes. It can spread aggressively by its roots and may outcompete other wildflowers in a small setting. The plant may die back in winter, particularly in North Florida.

OTHER SPECIES: Lakeside sunflower (*Helianthus carnosus*) blooms from late spring to fall with showy 3-inch yellow ray florets and greenish-yellow disk florets. The 1- to 3-foot bare stems rise from an evergreen basal rosette. Central and North Florida gardeners can use it in moist to wet soils. Use Lakeside sunflower in zones 8–9. Though it is endangered in Florida, it is easy to propagate, grow, and maintain in the garden and is available from native plant nurseries.

CAUTION: Narrowleaf sunflower naturally ranges as far west as Texas and as far north as New York. Large retail outlets and national seed suppliers sell varieties originating from out of state. Their performance in your landscape can be different than Florida ecotypes.

DUNE SUNFLOWER
(Helianthus debilis)

Dune sunflower occurs naturally along the coast but adapts well for inland use. Its bright flowers attract a variety of pollinators, including butterflies, moths, and bees. Its dense growth pattern provides cover for many small animals, while birds enjoy its seeds.

1–2 ft.

Blooms consist of brownish-red disk florets surrounded by yellow ray florets. Leaves are deltoid-shaped with rough surfaces and toothed margins. They are alternately arranged.

FAMILY: Asteraceae (aster, composite, or daisy family)

NATIVE RANGE: Dune sunflower has three subspecies: *H. debilis* subsp. *debilis* occurs on Florida's east coast; Cucumberleaf dune sunflower (*H. debilis* subsp. *cucumerifolius*) occurs in scattered Panhandle counties and a few peninsular ones; West coast dune sunflower (*H. debilis* subsp. *vestitus*) is endemic to Pinellas, Hillsborough, Manatee, Sarasota, Charlotte, and Lee counties.

LIFESPAN: Perennial

BLOOM SEASON: Summer; year-round in South Florida

GROWTH HABIT: 1–2' tall with 3–4'+ spread

PROPAGATION: Cuttings, seed. Allow flowerheads to dry on the plant then break open to collect seeds.

PLANTING: Plant in masses 3 to 4 feet apart and give it room to roam. Water seedlings only until established.

CARE: Plants get leggy and messy-looking over time. Light trims every three months keep foliage looking fresh. Periodically remove spent plants. Plants reseed readily; carefully dig up seedlings and relocate.

SITE CONDITIONS: Full sun to light shade; dry, well-drained sandy soils (avoid moist or heavily irrigated sites)

HARDINESS: Zones 8A–11A

GARDEN TIPS: Dune sunflower can tolerate salt and wind. Plant in full sun for best flowering. It is a prolific self-seeder and will spread quickly if not maintained. Depending on the variety, this plant may be spreading or upright. As a groundcover, it may sprawl several feet but generally is no more than 2 feet high. West coast dune sunflower can be taller.

CAUTION: Subspecies can hybridize and should not be planted together. In landscape or garden settings, the subspecies native to or appropriate for the region should be used. Environmentally conscientious gardeners living along the coast should ask their nursery for the subspecies native to their locale. This will help preserve the distinct identities and ecological roles of these plants.

STACEY MATRAZZO

RAYLESS SUNFLOWER
(Helianthus radula)

1–2 ft.

Rayless sunflower occurs naturally in pine flatwoods and seasonally wet savannahs and along moist to dry roadsides. It typically blooms late spring into early fall, attracting a wide variety of butterflies and other pollinators.

Each solitary flowerhead includes a compact but relatively large center composed of many small, dark maroon disk florets accented with yellow stamens. Ray florets are almost entirely absent. (Some specimens do produce a few small yellow ray florets.) Basal leaves are thick and rounded with a rough, hairy surface. Stem leaves are few, elliptic to ovate, and hairy and become reduced in size as they ascend the stem. They are oppositely arranged. Stems also are hairy.

The genus name *Helianthus* is from the Greek *hēlios*, or "sun," and *ánthos*, or "flower." The species epithet *radula* is from the Latin *radula*, meaning "scraper," referring to the roughness of the leaf surfaces.

FAMILY: Asteraceae (aster, composite, or daisy family)

NATIVE RANGE: Panhandle, most of North and Central Florida, and Collier County

LIFESPAN: Perennial

BLOOM SEASON: Late spring through early fall

GROWTH HABIT: 1–2' tall

PROPAGATION: Break apart seedhead and sow individual seeds.

PLANTING: Plants are available in 1-gallon containers. Space plants 1½ to 2 feet apart with other wildflowers or grasses.

CARE: Old flower stalks may be cut back to the basal rosettes after maturing. Be careful to not cover the rosette with mulch.

SITE CONDITIONS: Full sun to partial shade; somewhat dry to very moist sandy or loamy soils

HARDINESS: Zones 8A–9B

GARDEN TIPS: Appreciate Rayless sunflower for its unusual flowerheads and large basal leaves. It is a great addition to a home pollinator garden, as it is easily adaptable to a variety of conditions and will attract butterflies as well as other pollinators. Plant with a mix of wildflowers and grasses such as Chalky bluestem or Muhlygrass for a striking display.

SCARLET HIBISCUS
(Hibiscus coccineus)

3–7 ft.

Scarlet hibiscus, also known as Scarlet rosemallow, is an herbaceous to semi-woody perennial wildflower that is common along wetland and stream edges and in swamps and other wet, open sites. In summer it produces large crimson blooms that remain open only for a day. Scarlet hibiscus is a profuse bloomer, however, and will typically produce many flowers throughout the summer. Like other plants with deep red flowers, it is very attractive to hummingbirds, butterflies, and other pollinators.

Scarlet hibiscus flowers are large (4 to 8 inches in diameter) with five bright red petals, a five-lobed green calyx, and linear bracts. Flowers are born in leaf axils. Leaves are glabrous, palmate, and deeply lobed with long stalks. Margins are toothed, and leaf arrangement is alternate. Stems and petioles may be reddish. Seeds are born in ovoid five-celled capsules. Each cell may contain many seeds.

The genus name *Hibiscus* is from the Greek *hibiskos*, or "mallow." The species epithet *coccineus* is from the Greek *kókkinos*, meaning "scarlet red."

FAMILY: Malvaceae (mallow family)

NATIVE RANGE: Okaloosa County and eastern Panhandle, north and central peninsula, Collier and Broward counties

LIFESPAN: Perennial

BLOOM SEASON: Summer

GROWTH HABIT: 3–7'+ tall with 2–5' spread

PROPAGATION: Remove seeds from capsules and plant; seeds germinate easily.

PLANTING: Plants are available in 1- or 3-gallon containers. Plant about 3 feet apart.

CARE: Scarlet hibiscus will die back in the winter and should be pruned or cut back to the ground in the fall as it goes dormant.

SITE CONDITIONS: Full sun to partial shade; prefers moist to wet or inundated, rich soils but can be acclimated to well-drained soils with enough moisture. Add potted specimens to ponds or water features with low water levels.

HARDINESS: Zones 8A–11A

GARDEN TIPS: Scarlet hibiscus is one of our showiest native wildflowers. It is a great addition to any moist or wet landscape or areas that receive plenty of moisture.

KEITH BRADLEY

PRAIRIE IRIS
(Iris savannarum)

2–3 ft.

Prairie iris is an emergent aquatic with showy flowers that bloom in spring. It has one of America's largest native iris flowers. J. K. Small, an early Florida botanist, talks about colonies as far as the eye could see. It occurs naturally in swamps, wet prairies, and marshes and along the edges of rivers and ditches. Its seeds are eaten by birds.

The distinct whitish-blue to purple flowers of Prairie iris each have three petals and three sepals. The petals are narrow and mostly erect. The sepals are more recognizable and often mistaken for petals. They are longer (measuring 4 to 5 inches), spatulate with a pointed tip, downward-arching, and have a yellow to whitish "signal" or crest along their midribs. Several flowers usually occur on each flowering stem. Leaves are bright green, swordlike, and erect, standing up to 3 feet tall and overlapping at their base. Seeds are born in a three-parted capsule. Roots are fleshy and rhizomatous.

FAMILY: Iridaceae (iris family)

NATIVE RANGE: Eastern Panhandle south to Collier and Palm Beach counties

LIFESPAN: Perennial

BLOOM SEASON: Early spring

GROWTH HABIT: 2–3'+ feet tall

PROPAGATION: Division, seed

PLANTING: Plants are available in 1-gallon containers and sometimes as bare root stock. They should be planted in soils that are seasonally inundated or have shallow water levels. Space about 3 feet apart or closer for a quicker show. They also can be kept in containers or placed in water gardens.

CARE: Prairie iris blooms best in wet years or when the soil is very wet or shallowly inundated. Remove spent leaves, especially when kept in containers, or let leaves form mulch and decay.

SITE CONDITIONS: Full sun to partial shade; moist to wet or inundated, rich, acidic soils

HARDINESS: Zones 8A–10B

GARDEN TIPS: Prairie iris is an excellent plant for water features, lake edges, and retention ponds. Its spring-blooming flowers don't last long, but their ornamental beauty makes the plant well worth adding to wet gardens or landscapes. It colonizes via underground rhizomes and can spread aggressively if conditions are right.

KEITH BRADLEY

BLAZING STAR
(Liatris chapmanii, L. gracilis, L. spicata, L. laevigata)

2–4 ft.

Also known as Gayfeathers, Blazing stars light up our fall woods with lavender wands. Flowers start opening at the top of the stem and continue to bloom after cutting. They are excellent nectar plants and will reliably attract numerous butterflies, moths, bees, and other insect pollinators. Hummingbirds also may nectar on the flowers.

Florida gardeners will find four native *Liatris* species on the market that range from the driest sites to the wettest: Chapman's blazing star (*Liatris chapmanii*), Shortleaf blazing star (*L. laevigata*), Slender blazing star (*L. gracilis*), and Dense blazing star (*L. spicata*) (pictured).

Blazing stars are among our taller perennial wildflowers. One or more flowering stems rise from basal rosettes in the summer, with blooms appearing anywhere from late summer through fall, depending on the species. Flowers are composed of only tubular disk florets that vary in color from magenta to lavender to pale pinkish purple. They are born in wand-like spikes. Foliage tends to be thin or not particularly noticeable. These are deciduous wildflowers—they overwinter underground and send up stalks from thickened, corm- or bulb-like rootstock. Shortleaf blazing star maintains an evergreen basal rosette in the winter.

FAMILY: Asteraceae (aster, composite, or daisy family)

NATIVE RANGE: Throughout Florida

LIFESPAN: Perennial

BLOOM SEASON: Late summer and fall

GROWTH HABIT: 2–4'+ tall

PROPAGATION: Collect seed once the flowers are light tan in color and fluffy. Shake or lightly brush the flowers into a container. Cover seeds lightly with soil; they need light to germinate.

PLANTING: Blazing stars are available in 4-inch and gallon containers. Space plants 12 to 15 inches apart. Keep them watered until you see new growth or seasonal rains begin. You may plant from containers any time of year, even when plants are dormant.

CARE: Staking is only needed when plants have been over-irrigated or overfertilized and are weak from having grown too quickly. Cut stems only if necessary, and carefully, because plants pull up easily. Be very careful when weeding around them. You may want to mark plants so you remember where they are. After flowering, the dead stems shelter insects—an important food source for birds. Birds also feed on the seeds.

SITE CONDITIONS: Full sun; dry to moist, well-drained sandy soils

HARDINESS: Zones 8A–11A

GARDEN TIPS: Blazing stars require little ground space and can be used even in small gardens. To provide seasonal color and vertical interest, place plants in clusters in beds of mixed wildflowers and ornamental grasses. Blazing star's thin, stiff, upright silhouette is complemented by plants with rounder or spreading forms, wide strappy leaves, and different flower shapes and sizes.

CAUTION: Nonnative blazing stars are often sold in large retail stores and garden centers. Seed sold by out-of-state vendors is typically not Florida native ecotype.

MARY KEIM

CARDINALFLOWER
(Lobelia cardinalis)

2–5 ft.

Cardinalflower is an erect herbaceous wildflower that occurs naturally in floodplain forests, riverine swamps, and spring runs and along river and stream edges. In Florida, it is a threatened species. Its stunning scarlet flowers bloom summer through early winter. Hummingbirds are the primary pollinator, but the flowers also attract butterflies and bees.

Cardinalflower's brilliant red blooms are tubular and two-lipped, with wide-spreading petals that appear lobed but are actually fused. They are born in terminal spikes and bloom from bottom to top. The plant generally dies back to a basal rosette in winter. Leaves are deep green (sometimes with a reddish tinge) and elliptic to lanceolate. They have serrated margins and are alternately arranged. Stems are pubescent. The plant exudes a milky sap when broken. Seeds are born in small capsules.

The common name, Cardinalflower, has been in use since the mid-1600s and is likely derived from the flower's similarity to the robes worn by Catholic cardinals.

FAMILY: Campanulaceae (bellflower family)

NATIVE RANGE: Panhandle, north and central peninsula

LIFESPAN: Perennial

BLOOM SEASON: Summer through early winter

GROWTH HABIT: 2–5' tall

PROPAGATION: Division, seed. Large plants will produce pups that may be separated from the main plant and replanted. Seeds should be lightly scattered on moist peaty soils.

PLANTING: Plants are available in quart and 1-gallon containers. Choose a planting site with continuously moist or wet organic soil or even in shallow water. Space 1 to 2 feet apart in small clusters. Do not mulch over the rosette of leaves.

CARE: Cardinalflower may die back to the ground in winter or retain a rosette of leaves. Cut back the flowering stem after seed production or allow the seeds to scatter and reseed naturally.

SITE CONDITIONS: Full sun to partial shade; moist to wet, acidic, organic soils

HARDINESS: Zones 8A–10B

GARDEN TIPS: Cardinalflower is great for moist wildflower gardens, water gardens, and along edges of ponds, streams, and drainage depressions.

CAUTION: All parts of this plant are believed to be toxic if ingested. Cardinalflower ranges all the way to Canada and through the Midwest. Plants are best suited for Florida when purchased from local sources.

ELEANOR DIETRICH

SUNSHINE MIMOSA
(Mimosa strigillosa)

2–9 in.

Also known as Powderpuff, Sunshine mimosa is a prostrate, mat-forming wildflower that occurs naturally in open disturbed areas, along roadsides, and, infrequently, in pinelands and forests. It typically blooms spring through summer. Its showy pink to lavender flowers are pollinated mainly by bees but attract butterflies as well. It is the host plant for the Little sulphur butterfly.

Each pompom-like inflorescence is composed of many inconspicuous flowers that form a 1-inch globe. What is most visible are the prominent pink stamens topped with yellow anthers that give this plant its distinctive appearance. Flowerheads are born on long stalks that emerge from leaf axils. Leaves are bluish green and feather-like in appearance. They are bipinnately compound, having 15± pairs of linear leaflets. Stems are hairy and woody to herbaceous. Seeds are born in 1-inch-long rough pods.

Unlike its cousin, Sensitivebrier (*Mimosa quadrivalvis*), Sunshine mimosa does not climb or have hooked prickles. But like its cousin, its leaves fold up when touched.

FAMILY: Fabaceae (legume, bean, or pea family)

NATIVE RANGE: Nearly throughout peninsular Florida

LIFESPAN: Perennial

BLOOM SEASON: Spring and summer

GROWTH HABIT: 2–9" tall and spreading

PROPAGATION: Division, seed. Divide the plant where new roots have established.

PLANTING: The plant is available in quart and 1-gallon containers. It will spread to cover a large area, so spacing depends on how quickly coverage is desired. Though quite drought tolerant, it is slow to establish and needs adequate water during this time.

CARE: Cut back as needed to control it from spreading into unwanted areas.

SITE CONDITIONS: Full sun to minimal shade; dry to moist, well-drained sandy soils

HARDINESS: Zones 8A–10B

GARDEN TIPS: Sunshine mimosa is a great groundcover replacement. It is low growing, spreads readily, and tolerates mowing. It will not climb over other plants or structures, but it sprawls continuously and sets down roots as it grows. It is best to plant it in areas where obstacles will control its spread. It is a prolific bloomer and adaptable to both dry and moist sites.

SPOTTED BEEBALM
(*Monarda punctata*)

2–4 ft.

Spotted beebalm (also known as Dotted horsemint) is a robust, aromatic wildflower that occurs naturally along roadsides and in meadows, pinelands, and disturbed sites. It typically blooms late spring through fall, attracting a huge variety of pollinating insects, including bees, wasps, and butterflies. In winter, it dies back to the ground (in South Florida, to a basal rosette).

Its flowers are inconspicuous, hairy, and whitish yellow with purplish spots. Often mistaken for the flower are its showy, leaflike bracts that subtend its tiny flowers. Bracts vary in color from pink to lavender or purple and often have yellowish-green tips and undersides. Flowers are born in elongated spikes and arranged in whorls. Leaves are petiolate and pubescent with toothed margins. They are oppositely arranged. Stems are pubescent, erect, and square, like most members of the mint family. Seeds are born in nutlets at the base of each flower.

Spotted beebalm is high in thymol, which has antimicrobial, antifungal, and antiseptic properties and was used historically to treat ringworm and hookworm infections. When crushed, the leaves emit an oregano-like scent. The leaves can be brewed into a mild tea that is said to promote relaxation.

FAMILY: Lamiaceae (mint family)

NATIVE RANGE: Nearly throughout Florida

LIFESPAN: Perennial

BLOOM SEASON: Late spring through fall

GROWTH HABIT: 2–4' tall

PROPAGATION: Seed will germinate readily. Shake dried flowerheads to release seeds. Plants will also reseed on their own.

PLANTING: Plants are widely available in quart and 1-gallon containers. Plant about 2 feet apart in an area where plants can spread and where they will not dwarf or outcompete other wildflowers.

CARE: Occasional pruning of older growth and removal of spent plants is necessary. Plants will reseed readily, so cut back before seed sets or allow room for reseeding.

SITE CONDITIONS: Full sun to partial shade; dry to moist, well-drained soils

HARDINESS: Zones 8A–10A

GARDEN TIPS: Spotted beebalm has a long bloom time and can be a nice addition to a home landscape. Enjoy watching the diversity of pollinators it attracts.

FEAY'S PALAFOX AND COASTALPLAIN PALAFOX
(Palafoxia feayi, and P. integrifolia)

2–6 ft.

Feay's palafox is a unique wildflower, endemic only to Florida's central and southern peninsula. It occurs naturally in sandhills, scrubby flatwoods, and scrub. Coastalplain palafox is found in coastal hammocks, sandhills, and drier flatwoods. Both have flowers that are very attractive to a variety of butterflies and bees.

Although it is a member of the aster family, Feay's palafox (pictured, top) bears few visual similarities. It is more woody than herbaceous, its blooms are without petal-like ray florets, and its white-to-pinkish disk florets are tubular. Most noticeable are the dark purple to maroon-colored stigmas and the curved white styles that extend from the ends of each disk floret. At the base of each flower are bracts that vary from green to purple. Leaves are alternately arranged and oval-shaped toward the base. They get smaller and more linear toward the top of the plant. The leaf surface is rough to the touch. Seeds are born in inconspicuous achenes.

Coastalplain palafox (pictured, bottom) differs in that is not woody. Its pink and white flowers with prominent stigmas and curved styles give the plant a frilly appearance when in bloom.

FAMILY: Asteraceae (aster, composite, or daisy family)

NATIVE RANGE: Feay's palafox occurs in Central and South Florida; Coastalplain palafox occurs in the eastern Panhandle and throughout the peninsula.

LIFESPAN: Perennial

BLOOM SEASON: Late summer and early fall

GROWTH HABIT: Feay's palafox is 4–6'+ tall; Coastalplain palafox is 2–3' tall.

PROPAGATION: Seed

PLANTING: These gems are available in 1-gallon containers at a few native nurseries. Space about 18 inches apart in small masses or ideally mixed with bunchgrasses and other wildflowers.

CARE: Though both are perennials, Coastalplain palafox may die back in the winter. Remove spent plant parts at the end of the season to allow for new growth.

SITE CONDITIONS: Full sun to minimal shade; dry to somewhat moist, well-drained sandy soils

HARDINESS: Zones 8A–10B

GARDEN TIPS: The tendency of Feay's palafox to grow tall and lanky makes it best suited for larger plantings of wildflowers and grasses. Coastalplain palafox also works well in mixed wildflower gardens because it may become deciduous.

MANYFLOWER BEARDTONGUE
(Penstemon multiflorus)

3–4 ft.

Manyflower beardtongue (also known as White beard-tongue) is a perennial wildflower. It blooms in spring and summer and occurs naturally in scrub, sandhills, and scrubby flatwoods. Manyflower beardtongue is almost endemic to Florida, with only a few populations in Alabama and Georgia. It attracts a number of pollinators, including hummingbirds, and is the host plant for the Baltimore checkerspot.

The plant's showy white to light lavender blooms are born in terminal panicles on oppositely arranged stalks. Each flower is tube-shaped with five lobes. Calyces also are five-lobed and hairy. Stems are erect, reddish in color, and emerge from a basal rosette of large grayish-green leaves. Stem leaves are sessile and oblong to lanceolate with entire or slightly toothed margins. They are oppositely arranged and become reduced as they ascend the stem.

The species epithet *multiflorus* is from the Latin *multus*, or "many," and *florus*, or "flower," and refers to the many flowers born on each flower stalk. The common epithet "beardtongue" refers to the tendency of blooms within the *Penstemon* genus to have a long, often hairy filament that protrudes from the mouth of the corolla, giving the appearance of a fuzzy tongue.

FAMILY: Plantaginaceae (plantain family)

NATIVE RANGE: Nearly throughout Florida

LIFESPAN: Perennial

BLOOM SEASON: Spring and summer

GROWTH HABIT: 3–4' tall

PROPAGATION: Seed. Collect from matured flowering stems; sow on the surface of well-drained soils.

PLANTING: Plants are available in 1-gallon containers. Plant about 2 feet apart.

CARE: Cut stems back to basal rosette after blooming and seed dispersal. Plants may die back to the ground in North Florida.

SITE CONDITIONS: Full sun to minimal shade; moist, well-drained sandy soils

HARDINESS: Zones 8A–10A

GARDEN TIPS: Manyflower beardtongue works well in wild or naturalistic settings as well more formal gardens. Masses of these tall, white bloom stalks are a showstopper. The plant spreads on its own by reseeding and by producing "pups" from the main rosette.

MARY KEIM

FROGFRUIT
(Phyla nodiflora)

2–3 in.

Frogfruit is known by many names, including Turkey tangle frogfruit, Capeweed, Matchhead, Creeping Charlie, and Carpetweed. Regardless of what you call it, it is both a versatile and vital wildflower. It is a good nectar source for bees and small butterflies, such as hairstreaks, and is the host plant for the White peacock, Phaon crescent, and Common buckeye butterflies. It occurs naturally in hammocks, beaches, and lawns and along roadsides. This evergreen perennial is low growing and creeping, often forming a dense mat of green foliage. Its distinct white-and-purple flowers are small but very showy, particularly when massed.

Frogfruit's distinct yet tiny flowers are composed of several to many white to pinkish flowers surrounding a dark purple center. They are born on relatively long erect stalks, giving the appearance of little matchsticks, hence the common name "Matchhead." Leaves are petiolate and elliptic to oval with tapered bases and toothed margins near the tips. They are oppositely arranged. Stems are generally prostrate.

FAMILY: Verbenaceae (verbena family)

NATIVE RANGE: Throughout Florida

LIFESPAN: Perennial

BLOOM SEASON: Year-round

GROWTH HABIT: 2–3"+

PROPAGATION: Cuttings, division

PLANTING: Plants usually are available in quart or 1-gallon containers. Place in moist soil where they can spread, spacing 2 feet or more apart to achieve cover.

CARE: Provide consistent soil moisture until established. Plants can sometimes be stippled with small insect damage,

but it does not usually need to be controlled.

SITE CONDITIONS: Full sun to partial shade; moist sandy, clay, or loamy soils

HARDINESS: Zones 8A–11A

GARDEN TIPS: Frogfruit makes a great groundcover, as it can form dense mats in the right conditions. It also works well in a hanging basket. Because the plant spreads and roots at nodes, it can be easily grown from cuttings or by division. Frogfruit has a moderately high salt and wind tolerance, making it a good plant for Florida's coastal areas. It is especially valuable as a larval and nectar plant to draw butterflies.

WILD PENNYROYAL
(Piloblephis rigida)

1–2 ft.

Wild pennyroyal is a low growing, evergreen, herbaceous to semi-woody perennial. It typically flowers in late winter through spring but can bloom year-round. It occurs naturally in scrub, scrubby and pine flatwoods, sandhills, dry prairies, and ruderal areas. Except for a small population in Georgia, it is endemic to Florida. Its flowers are attractive to a variety of bees and butterflies. Because of its early bloom period, it supplies pollen and nectar when little else is available, making it an important part of natural landscaping and restoration areas.

Wild pennyroyal's small, two-lipped flowers may be lavender, purple, or pinkish. Lower lips are lobed with dark purple spots. Stamens are prominent. Flowers are born in dense cone-shaped terminal clusters. Sepals are pubescent and green with purple margins. Leaves are tiny and needlelike with entire margins. They are oppositely arranged. Stems are semi-woody to woody and branched. The fruit is a small aggregate of four nutlets.

Piloblephis rigida is the only species in its genus. The genus name *Piloblephis* comes from the Greek *pilo*, or "hairy," and *blephis*, or "eyelid," and refers to the tiny soft hairs that coat the sepals. The species epithet *rigida* is from the Latin *rigidus*, meaning "rigid," and refers to its stiff branches.

The entire plant is delightfully aromatic, particularly when crushed. Like most members of the mint family, it has a minty smell, although the scent may be more lemony in some populations. Its leaves can be brewed into a minty tea.

FAMILY: Lamiaceae (mint family)

NATIVE RANGE: Peninsular Florida

LIFESPAN: Perennial

BLOOM SEASON: Late winter and spring, but may bloom year-round

GROWTH HABIT: 1–2' tall and equally broad

PROPAGATION: Sow seeds in pots and transplant. Cuttings are possible but usually require a mist system.

PLANTING: Plants are available in 1-gallon containers. Plant in groups or mix with other wildflowers. Space 12 to 24 inches apart.

CARE: Wild pennyroyal does well in nutrient-poor soils but needs adequate moisture to establish.

SITE CONDITIONS: Full sun; dry, well-drained sandy soils

HARDINESS: Zones 8B–10B

GARDEN TIPS: Wild pennyroyal can be mixed with other wildflowers in a garden setting and in butterfly and pollinator gardens. It is drought tolerant.

MARY KEIM

NARROWLEAF SILKGRASS
(Pityopsis tracyi)

1–2 ft.

Narrowleaf silkgrass, also known as Grass-leaved golden-aster or Silver-leaved aster, is found throughout peninsular Florida in scrub, scrubby flatwoods, and pine flatwoods ecosystems. At first glance and when not in bloom, the plant may appear to be a grass. Its flowers attract butterflies and various pollinators.

Flowers are compound with many bright yellow ray florets surrounding a compact center of orangish-yellow disk florets. The plant's mostly basal leaves are long, linear, and grasslike. They are covered in fine hairs, giving the leaves a silvery hue. Stem leaves are short by comparison, appressed, and alternately arranged. Seeds are born in achenes.

The genus name *Pityopsis* is from the Greek *pitys*, or "pine." It is a reference to the nymph Pitys, who, in Greek mythology, was changed into a pine tree by the gods.

FAMILY: Asteraceae (aster, composite, or daisy family)

NATIVE RANGE: Peninsular Florida from Duval County south

LIFESPAN: Perennial

BLOOM SEASON: Late fall and early winter

GROWTH HABIT: 1' tall; 2' tall when blooming

PROPAGATION: Division, seed. Collect once flowering has completed and seed has fluffed out. Seeds are not viable for long; sow soon after harvesting or protect from heat and humidity.

PLANTING: Plants are available in quart or gallon containers. Space them 2 feet apart, closer if your intention is to quickly establish as a groundcover.

CARE: After the plants have bloomed, cut back the flowering stems to ground level if desired or leave seed for wildlife. Where Narrowleaf silkgrass has been used as a groundcover, plants can be mowed or cut back to the ground; use well-sharpened blades, as the stems and leaves are quite tough.

SITE CONDITIONS: Full sun to light shade; dry to moist, well-drained sandy or calcareous soils

HARDINESS: Zones 8A–11A

GARDEN TIPS: Narrowleaf silkgrass is relatively easy to establish and maintain over time. Its silky foliage can make a dense groundcover in dry to moist soils. The plant spreads by underground rhizomes; a single plant can spread and densely cover a much larger area.

PICKERELWEED
(Pontederia cordata)

2–4 ft.

Pickerelweed is a long-lived perennial aquatic wildflower that occurs naturally in open aquatic habitats such as pond, lake, or river edges, marshes, and swamps. Pickerelweed typically blooms spring through fall. It is pollinated primarily by bees but is visited by many butterflies and other insects. Its seeds are eaten by birds. Ducks also are known to eat the entire plant.

Pickerelweed's conspicuous blooms are born in erect, showy spikes. Flowers are tubular with deep purplish-blue petals and yellow or white markings that may serve as nectar guides for bees. Flower spikes extend above all but one leaf, which grows just below and behind the spike. Leaves are sagittate with a long, tapering blade and a cordate base (hence the species epithet *cordata*). They are dark green and alternately arranged. The fruit is an achene that bears a single inconspicuous seed.

Pickerelweed seeds, stalks, and leaves are edible to humans. Seeds can be eaten raw, boiled, or roasted. Young leaves and stalks can be eaten raw or boiled.

FAMILY: Pontederiaceae

NATIVE RANGE: Nearly throughout Florida

LIFESPAN: Perennial

BLOOM SEASON: Spring through fall, with heaviest bloom in late spring

GROWTH HABIT: 2–4' tall

PROPAGATION: Division, seed. Divide young plants in spring.

PLANTING: Plants are available as bare-root specimens and in 1-gallon containers. Plant in water 2 to 12 inches deep and where water levels will not fluctuate to more than 2 feet but soil will remain saturated. Space 3 to 4 feet apart and allow the plants to spread.

CARE: No special care is needed. As plant parts die, they sink below water and decay. Plants will spread to a water depth they can tolerate, or control to desired limits.

SITE CONDITIONS: Full sun to partial shade; acidic to neutral, inundated to saturated soils

HARDINESS: Zones 8A–10B

GARDEN TIPS: Pickerelweed is great for water gardens as well as for pond edges and drainage swales, where it can help with soil stabilization. It flowers best if grown in full sun. It is fast-growing and spreads easily on its own by underground rhizomes, forming large colonies if not maintained.

MARY KEIM

BLACK-EYED SUSAN
(Rudbeckia hirta)

1–2 ft.

Black-eyed Susan is found throughout Florida in sand-hills, flatwoods, and disturbed areas. It is an excellent nectar source for a variety of butterflies and bees and is also a larval host to some moths. The seeds are eaten by birds.

Black-eyed Susan's compound flowerhead consists of many long yellow ray florets surrounding a central dome of dark purple to brown disk florets. Each solitary flowerhead is born on a rough, erect stem that emerges from a basal rosette of bristly leaves. Stem leaves are alternately arranged, with toothed margins and rough surfaces. Seeds are tiny black achenes.

Cut flowers can last up to 10 days in bouquets. Black-eyed Susan roots have also been used in various medicines.

FAMILY: Asteraceae (aster, composite, or daisy family)

NATIVE RANGE: Throughout Florida

LIFESPAN: Depending on the conditions, Black-eyed Susan can generally perform as a short-lived perennial, biennial, or annual. A perennial variety, *Rudbeckia hirta* var. *floridana*, occurs in Central and South Florida.

BLOOM SEASON: Spring through fall; may bloom in winter in Central and South Florida

GROWTH HABIT: 1–2' tall

PROPAGATION: Collect seed after the ray and disk flowers finish blooming and have dried slightly. Pick a head and tear it apart to find the mature cone-shaped seeds, which should have solid white centers.

PLANTING: Plants are generally available in quart and gallon containers. Space them 14 to 18 inches apart.

CARE: Monitor plants during extra-long dry periods, especially in spring, and water deeply only as needed. Black-eyed Susan flowers can be cut after they bloom to encourage more flowering stems and lengthen the bloom period.

SITE CONDITIONS: Full sun to partial shade; somewhat dry to moist, well-drained sandy soils

HARDINESS: Zones 8A–11A

GARDEN TIPS: Black-eyed Susans are easy to grow and maintain. They spread by way of abundant self-sown seed. They are adaptable to both semidry and moist sites but flower best with regular moisture. They are excellent for mixed wildflower gardens and disturbed areas such as roadsides and medians.

CAUTION: There are many named cultivars of *Rudbeckia* species, and some are quite popular and widely available. None of the cultivars currently available were derived from Florida ecotypes, and they are not considered native wildflowers. They may not perform as well or live as long as those from your local region.

WILD PETUNIA
(Ruellia caroliniensis)

Wild petunia is a long-lived perennial wildflower found in sandhills, flatwoods, and moist to wet hammocks. The lavender-blue corollas attract a variety of bees, including bumble, leafcutter, and honey bees. Several butterfly species, including the White peacock, Malachite, and Mangrove buckeye, gather nectar from the flowers. The plant is a host for the Common buckeye.

6–18 in.

Flowers are five-petaled, funnel-shaped, and grow to about 2 inches in diameter. They are born in clusters along multibranched stems. Leaves are green, simple, and ovate to elliptic with opposite arrangement. Like other members of the Acanthaceae family, Wild petunia's mature seed capsules will explode open, sending seeds far from the parent plant. The plant has many growth habits, from prostrate to erect and with short or long internodes.

Although the common name is "petunia," the flowers in the *Ruellia* genus are not true petunias, which are members of the Solanaceae (nightshade) family.

FAMILY: Acanthaceae (acanthus family)

NATIVE RANGE: Nearly throughout Florida

LIFESPAN: Perennial

BLOOM SEASON: Spring through fall; year-round in warmer climes

GROWTH HABIT: 6–18" tall

PROPAGATION: Cuttings, seed

PLANTING: Plants are widely available in various pot sizes and can be planted throughout the growing season. Plant 12 to 15 inches apart, or grow in a hanging basket or large, well-drained container.

CARE: Wild petunia may be trimmed halfway through its growing season to promote new growth and blooms. Remove three or four internodes (4 to 6 inches) with scissors or clippers. Annual pruning may be required to remove old stems.

SITE CONDITIONS: Full sun to fairly dense shade; prefers dry to moist, well-drained soils but has been known to grow in wet, mucky soils

HARDINESS: Zones 8A–10B

GARDEN TIPS: Wild petunia does well in a mixed wildflower bed of plants and grasses. Its showy flowers last only a day, but successional blooms keep the plant looking fresh. Establishing Wild petunia in shadier locations will result in plants that appear lanky with fewer blooms. In North Florida it is not recommended for mass plantings, as it will die back in the winter, leaving a patch of stems.

CAUTION: Although the nursery industry offers some sterile nonnative *Ruellia* species, the widely grown Mexican petunia (*Ruellia simplex*; synonyms *R. brittoniana* and *R. tweediana*) should be avoided, as it may reproduce via underground rhizomes. As a Category I invasive exotic species, it has spread into municipal and natural areas, displacing native species and changing community structures or ecological functions.

SCARLET SAGE AND LYRELEAF SAGE
(Salvia coccinea, and S. lyrata)

12–36 in.

Scarlet sage (*Salvia coccinea*) and Lyreleaf sage (*S. lyrata*) are widespread wildflowers found in thickets and disturbed sites and along roadsides. Both are excellent nectar sources for butterflies and bumblebees. Hummingbirds are attracted to Scarlet sage.

The abundant blooms of Scarlet sage (pictured, top) are 1 inch long and usually deep coral or fire-engine red, although pink and white forms occur as well. The plant's square stems are green to dark brown. For much of the year, Lyreleaf sage (pictured, bottom) consists of relatively flat, variegated leaves that display a range of green, dark violet, and chocolate brown. Light violet-colored flowers appear on deep green or burgundy-colored stems.

Salvia has a long history of medicinal uses. Crush the foliage, and you'll detect a faint herbal fragrance.

FAMILY: Lamiaceae (mint family)

NATIVE RANGE: Scarlet sage occurs throughout much of Florida. Lyreleaf sage occurs in all but the southeastern-most counties.

LIFESPAN: Perennial

BLOOM SEASON: Summer through fall (Scarlet sage; may bloom year-round in Central and South Florida); late winter and spring (Lyreleaf sage)

GROWTH HABIT: 18–36" tall (Scarlet sage) and 12–24" tall (Lyreleaf sage) for flowering stems

PROPAGATION: Cuttings, division, seed. Allow flowers to dry on stems, and gently shake them into a container to obtain seed.

PLANTING: Plants are available in 4-inch to 1-gallon containers. Space Scarlet sage 1 to 2 feet apart. They self-seed readily and will spread throughout the garden. Plant Lyreleaf sage in small clusters, placing plants about a foot apart.

CARE: For continuous blooming, cut back Scarlet sage's spent flowers. Lyreleaf sage can be mowed in late spring or early summer after it seeds. It may need water if planted in full sun or during extended drought.

SITE CONDITIONS: Scarlet sage does best in full sun to afternoon shade. Lyreleaf sage prefers partial shade but will tolerate sun. Both do best in moderately dry to moist, well-drained sandy soils.

HARDINESS: Zones 8A–10B

GARDEN TIPS: Use Scarlet sage in a mixed wildflower bed or as an accent by itself. Some growers have successfully established Lyreleaf sage as a spreading groundcover after two or three years of cultivation in a landscape. It also does well as a groundcover under oaks if the soil is moderately moist.

HELMET SKULLCAP
(Scutellaria integrifolia)

12–18 in.

Helmet skullcap is a diminutive yet showy wildflower that occurs naturally in sandhills, pine flatwoods, and upland mixed forests, as well as along marsh and swamp edges. It typically blooms in late spring and summer, attracting a wide range of bees, including leafcutter, cuckoo, and bumble bees. A few butterflies, such as the Gulf fritillary, Spicebush swallowtail, and Eastern black swallowtail, sporadically visit the flower.

Helmet skullcap's lavender to violet flowers are two-lipped and resemble snapdragon blooms. The lower lip consists of three fused lobes with a white splotch extending down the throat. Upper petals are fused and curved, forming a small hood or helmetlike structure. Flowers are born on terminal racemes in the axils of the bract-like upper leaves. The plant begins as a basal rosette of bright green arrow-shaped leaves with coarsely toothed margins. From the rosette, many branched stems emerge. Stem leaves vary from elliptical to arrow-shaped and are oppositely arranged. Upper leaves are narrower and have entire margins. Seeds are small, shiny, and black and are produced in nutlets.

The genus name *Scutellaria* is from the Latin *scutella*, or "dish," possibly describing the lower platelike petal. The species epithet *integrifolia* refers to its smooth leaf margins.

FAMILY: Lamiaceae (mint family)

NATIVE RANGE: Throughout Florida, except southernmost counties

LIFESPAN: Perennial

BLOOM SEASON: Late spring and summer

GROWTH HABIT: 12–18" tall

PROPAGATION: Harvest seed when nutlet coat turns light brown and papery. The plant may hold flowers and seeds at the same time. Germination may take up to 30 days.

PLANTING: Plants are generally available in 1-gallon containers. Space 12 to 18 inches apart.

CARE: Helmet skullcap readily spreads by seed. Excess seedlings can be easily removed or transplanted. To avoid having to weed out seedlings, prune plants back after flowering to limit seed production. Disease and pests are not a problem with this wildflower. Plants die back to a basal rosette in winter.

SITE CONDITIONS: Full sun to light shade; dry to moist, well-drained sandy soils

HARDINESS: Zones 8A–9B

GARDEN TIPS: Helmet skullcap is ideal for a mixed wildflower bed or wildflower border, or within a pond or rock garden. Plants will be dormant in winter, dying back to the rootstock. Helmet skullcap is not salt tolerant.

PEG URBAN

STARRY ROSINWEED
(Silphium asteriscus)

Starry rosinweed is a robust wildflower that occurs naturally in flatwoods, sandy pinelands, and disturbed areas. Its bright, showy flowers attract a variety of butterflies, native bees, and other pollinators. Birds will eat its seeds.

2–5 ft.

Flowerheads are large—up to 2½ inches in diameter. They are composed of many bright yellow ray florets surrounding a center of yellow to green disk florets. Flowerheads are born on branched stems and supported by an involucre of large bracts. Leaves are lanceolate with toothed margins and rough surfaces. Seeds are born in winged achenes.

The common name "rosinweed" refers to the gummy or resinous substance found in the stems. Native Americans chewed stems to clean their teeth. Rosinweeds have a long history of medicinal uses in North America and Europe.

FAMILY: Asteraceae (aster, composite, or daisy family)

NATIVE RANGE: Panhandle and western central peninsula south to Lee County

LIFESPAN: Perennial

BLOOM SEASON: Spring through early fall (year-round if temperatures are mild)

GROWTH HABIT: 2–5' tall

PROPAGATION: Collect seeds when flowerheads are dry. Break apart to separate seeds. For best results, plant seeds shortly after collection and keep soil surface moist. If seeds are stored, keep them at a low humidity and temperature and sow when ready.

PLANTING: Plants are generally available in 1-gallon containers. Space plants about 2 feet apart. Water deeply and thoroughly to wet the soil at least 7 inches down until the plant is established, but only as often as needed.

CARE: In the right soils and once established, plants should not need additional watering. However, plants should be monitored during long spring droughts. Flowering stems may be cut back to encourage more flowering. Plants also will readily reseed.

SITE CONDITIONS: Full sun to partial shade; moderately dry to moist, well-drained soils

HARDINESS: Zones 8A–10B

GARDEN TIPS: Starry rosinweed is especially loved because it blooms heavily over a long period of time. The plant will persist in the landscape, although it may die back in the winter, and can reseed on its own. Although its natural range is the west side of the peninsula, it performs well through much of the state.

BLUE-EYED GRASS
(Sisyrinchium angustifolium)

6–12 in.

Blue-eyed grass is an evergreen, clump-forming wildflower found in wet flatwoods, wet prairies, and moist open habitats throughout Florida. The flowers attract a variety of pollinators, including bumblebees, sweat bees, and other native bees and flies. Birds eat the seeds.

Its dainty star-shaped flowers are born atop flat grasslike stems. Tepals are blue but may appear purple or lavender, especially in photos. They darken as they near the center of the flower, which is bright yellow. They have obvious venation, are tipped with sharp points, and arch back toward the stem as the flower opens. Flowers generally open around noon in sunny conditions and close at the end of the day. Leaves are long, linear, flattened, and basal. Seeds develop in capsules that wrinkle and turn dark brown as they mature.

The grasslike appearance of both stems and leaves give Blue-eyed grass its common name. However, it is in no way related to the grass family.

FAMILY: Iridaceae (iris family)

NATIVE RANGE: Throughout Florida

LIFESPAN: Perennial

BLOOM SEASON: Late winter and spring (generally blooming for a two-month period)

GROWTH HABIT: 6–12" tall

PROPAGATION: Division, seed

PLANTING: Plants are available in quart or 1-gallon containers. Space 12 to 15 inches apart in moist sandy soils without organic amendments for ideal growth and less competition from weedy plants. Plant anytime.

CARE: Keep other plants and weeds out of new plantings, as Blue-eyed grass's low, flat form can be easily overcome. Avoid fertilizers and other organics, as they will encourage competition.

SITE CONDITIONS: Full sun; moderately dry, moist, or wet sandy, loamy, or calcareous soils

HARDINESS: Zones 8A–11A

GARDEN TIPS: The low profile of Blue-eyed grass makes it an excellent groundcover that will provide a carpet of green throughout the year and masses of blue flowers in spring. Planting in full sun and moist sandy soil will result in denser foliage and more flowers, but it is somewhat adaptable to drier and shadier conditions. It also will spread by underground rhizomes to create fuller stands, but is not an aggressive spreader.

SEASIDE GOLDENROD
(Solidago sempervirens)

4–6 ft.

Seaside goldenrod is generally the most available of the four native goldenrods that are grown commercially. It blooms in very showy masses on dunes, in swales and brackish marshes, on sandy soils in coastal areas, and occasionally inland throughout the state. Its nectar attracts a variety of butterflies, bees, and other pollinators. The plant also attracts birds searching for insects.

Seaside goldenrod has golden-yellow tubular blooms that densely cover long inflorescences born on the tips of the stem. It retains its long strap-shaped, somewhat-fleshy basal leaves year-round. Leaves gradually become smaller as they ascend stems.

Goldenrod is often mistakenly blamed for triggering allergies, but it is ragweed, which blooms heavily around the same time, that is actually to blame. Goldenrods have been used medicinally since Roman times or earlier. Seaside goldenrod was used by Seminoles to treat wounds.

FAMILY: Asteraceae (aster, composite, or daisy family)

NATIVE RANGE: Coastal Panhandle, most peninsular counties

LIFESPAN: Annual/perennial

BLOOM SEASON: Summer and fall (spring through fall in South Florida)

GROWTH HABIT: 1–2' tall; 4–6' when in bloom

PROPAGATION: Division, seed. Collect seeds after flowers are spent and fluffy pappus appear.

PLANTING: Plants are available in quart, 1-gallon, and 3-gallon containers. Because of their large size, they can be spaced 3 feet or more apart and allowed to fill in over time.

CARE: This plant performs best in harsh conditions with no watering after establishment. To reduce height, cut back plants in midsummer before blooms start to form, and cut back to basal rosettes after blooming.

SITE CONDITIONS: Full sun to minimal shade; moist, well-drained sandy soils

HARDINESS: Zones 8A–11A

GARDEN TIPS: Seaside goldenrod is easy to retain in the landscape. It spreads by rhizomes to make dense colonies over time. Plant it where it can make a big show in the garden, or allow it a large space in the landscape. It needs lots of sun to bloom prolifically, but it will tolerate some shade. Seaside goldenrod is salt tolerant.

OTHER SPECIES: Wand goldenrod (*Solidago stricta*) blooms in the fall in wetter flatwoods and prairie communities throughout Florida. This 2- to 4-foot perennial has small basal leaves and very small appressed leaves on its flowering stems, which die back after seeds mature. The plant has a slender wand-like appearance similar to blazing stars that bloom at the same time. Chapman's goldenrod (*Solidago odora* var. *chapmanii*) likes the dry sandy soils of sandhills and open hammocks in the peninsula and a few areas in the central Panhandle. It does not spread by rhizomes and has multiple woody branches that grow to 3 and 4 feet tall—shorter than most other species. Its typical golden flowers bloom in late summer to early fall and are found on the tips of downward-bending branches.

BLUE PORTERWEED
(Stachytarpheta jamaicensis)

1–3 ft.

Blue porterweed is a low growing and sprawling wild-flower. Found in coastal dunes, shell mounds, and disturbed areas, it typically flowers in the summer but may flower year-round in South Florida. It is an excellent addition to a butterfly garden, as it is the host plant for the Tropical buckeye and is a nectar source for many butterfly species, including the Clouded skipper, Gulf fritillary, Red admiral, and Julia.

Blue porterweed's diminutive tubular flowers are purplish blue with a white "eye." They are born on long, narrow spikes. Flowers open for only one day and won't open on very cloudy days. Leaves are dark green and ovate to lanceolate with serrated margins. They are oppositely arranged. Stems are branched and angled. Seeds are inconspicuous nutlets.

The genus name *Stachytarpheta* is from the Greek *stachys*, meaning "spike," and *tarphys*, meaning "thick" or "dense."

FAMILY: Verbenaceae (verbena family)

NATIVE RANGE: South Florida, east Central Florida, Hillsborough and Wakulla counties

LIFESPAN: Perennial

BLOOM SEASON: Summer; year-round in South Florida

GROWTH HABIT: 1–3' tall with 2–3' spread

PROPAGATION: Cuttings, seed

PLANTING: Plants are available in 1- and 3-gallon containers. Space 2 to 3 feet apart in masses or mixed with other wildflowers. Plant in a protected area if using north of its typical range.

CARE: Trim plants as needed to keep size in check.

SITE CONDITIONS: Full sun to minimal shade; dry to moist well-drained sandy, clay, loamy, or calcareous soils

HARDINESS: Zones 9B–11A

GARDEN TIPS: Blue porterweed is drought tolerant, moderately salt tolerant, and does well in poor soil. Its low growing habit makes it a nice groundcover in dry, sunny areas. It also does well in a container or in a mixed wildflower garden.

CAUTION: The nonnative *Stachytarpheta cayennensis* is often mistaken for the native species, as both have distinctive purplish-blue flowers. The Florida Exotic Pest Plant Council (FLEPPC) recognizes *S. cayennensis* as a Category II invasive species because it has escaped cultivation and is altering native habitat. It should not be used.

MARY KEIM

CLIMBING ASTER
(Symphyotrichum carolinianum)

5–8 ft.

Climbing aster is a sprawling vine-like shrub that occurs naturally in coastal hammocks and wet flatwoods and along the edges of swamps, springs, and streams. As a late fall- and winter-flowering species, it helps extend the options for nectar and pollen available to pollinators. It is one of the few wildflowers that will bloom in December. Flowers draw myriad native bees, including polyester, sweat, cuckoo, leafcutter, mining, bumble, and miner bees. Butterflies and moths also love them: Monarchs, Pearl crescents, skippers, fritillaries, Common buckeyes, Gray hairstreaks, swallowtails, and sulphurs have been known to frequent the flowers for nectar.

The compound flowers have dense centers of yellow–orange disk florets surrounded by many ray florets that vary in color from lavender to purplish pink to violet. Flowers are 1 to 2 inches in diameter and have a very sweet fragrance. Leaves are grayish green and elliptic to ovate with entire margins and are born alternately on branches. The seed is an achene with a fluffy pappus.

FAMILY: Asteraceae (aster, composite, or daisy family)

NATIVE RANGE: All of Florida except western Panhandle

LIFESPAN: Perennial

BLOOM SEASON: Late fall and early winter (year-round in favorable conditions)

GROWTH HABIT: 8'+ long if climbing; 5' tall and wide if self-standing

PROPAGATION: Sow seed in late fall or winter.

PLANTING: Plants are available in 1- and 3-gallon containers. For masses of plants, space 3 or more feet apart. Plant where it can roam free or stand alone.

CARE: Cut back Climbing aster in late winter after flowering to encourage future blooms and healthy growth and to limit size, or simply let it ramble.

SITE CONDITIONS: Full sun to partial shade; somewhat dry to moist sandy, loamy, or organic soils

HARDINESS: Zones 8A–11A

GARDEN TIPS: The sprawling nature of Climbing aster makes it suitable for growing along a trellis or fence. It also can be placed on slopes near the edge of ponds, lakes, or streams or at the bases of wetland trees. Though a wetland species, it does well with less soil moisture and can even be used as a standalone shrub. In formal landscapes, it can take on a tangled or chaotic appearance; however, it can be pruned to any shape.

GIANT IRONWEED
(Vernonia gigantea)

3–5 ft.

Giant ironweed is a robust, perennial wildflower found naturally in floodplains, wet to mesic pine flatwoods, and ruderal areas and along forest margins and stream banks. Flowering occurs in summer and fall, attracting a variety of pollinators, especially butterflies.

Unlike many members of the aster family, the Giant ironweed flower lacks ray florets. Its disc florets are tubular and deep purple. Extending from within each disc floret tube is a bifurcated and curled style. Flowers are about 1 inch in diameter and are born in loose terminal panicles. At the base of each flower are bracts that vary in color from dark green to purplish green to brown. Basal leaves are coarse, oval-shaped, and appear in early spring. Stem leaves are narrowly ovate to elliptic and can grow up to 8 inches long. Both have serrated margins. Stems may be glabrous or finely pubescent. Seeds are tiny achenes with tufts of bristles that catch the wind and aid in dispersal.

The common name "ironweed" may refer to the toughness of the stem of this and other *Vernonia* species.

FAMILY: Asteraceae (aster, composite, or daisy family)

NATIVE RANGE: Panhandle and peninsula south to Martin and Lee counties

LIFESPAN: Perennial

BLOOM SEASON: Summer and fall

GROWTH HABIT: 3–5' tall

PROPAGATION: Division, seed. Separate "pups" from the main plant and replant. Sow seed and cover very lightly with soil.

PLANTING: Plants are available in 1-gallon containers. Plant 18 inches or more apart in semi-shady to sunny spots where the height can be appreciated.

CARE: Giant ironweed can sucker and may require weeding to contain it. It is deciduous and will die back in the winter, at which time dead foliage may be trimmed.

SITE CONDITIONS: Full sun to partial shade; moderately dry to moist, well-drained sandy or loamy soils

HARDINESS: Zones 8A–10B

GARDEN TIPS: Giant ironweed is very adaptable in the landscape, although it is not drought tolerant. It is an excellent addition to a butterfly or mixed wildflower garden, but it is best located in the back of the planting due to its height.

Flowering Vines

FLOWERING VINES ARE A GREAT WAY to add vertical interest to your landscape, particularly when surface space is limited. They are typically fast-growing plants that clamber, cling, and climb their way to the sky in search of sunlight. This rambling growth habit forms a dense network of stems and leaves that provides nesting habitat and protective cover for wildlife. Many vines produce nectar-rich tubular flowers that attract hummingbirds and large insects, and juicy berries that offer a tasty treat for birds and other wildlife. Vines can't support themselves naturally, so they typically seek out trees, shrubs, or other natural supports on which to climb. When adding vines to your garden, place them at the base of a fence, trellis, or other structure, where they will be supported and allowed to freely spread. Their climbing habit enables them to take over an area quite quickly, which may be challenging to manage. However, most vines can be pruned to control their growth and maintain a desired size or form. Some also make attractive groundcovers.

TRUMPET CREEPER
(Campsis radicans)

30 ft.

Trumpet creeper is a high-climbing woody vine so named because its showy flowers are trumpet-shaped. It is found in moist woodlands and thickets throughout Central and North Florida. Flowers bloom year-round, peaking in spring and summer. They are very attractive to hummingbirds.

Trumpet creeper's flowers are long, tubular, and reddish orange with a yellowish throat. They are born in terminal cymes. Leaves are dark green, pinnately compound, and fernlike. Leaflets, which number at least seven per leaf, are ovate to lanceolate with serrated margins and pointed tips. Leaves and leaflets are oppositely arranged. The plant climbs via aerial rootlets. Tendrils are lacking, and the stem is woody and robust. Trumpet creeper's fruit is a long (3 to 5 inches) bean-like capsule bearing many winged seeds.

Flowers are very similar in appearance to the flowers of its cousin, Crossvine (*Bignonia capreolata*). The latter has visible tendrils and its compound leaves have only two leaflets.

The species epithet *radicans* comes from the Latin *radix*, or "root," and refers to the plant's motility via its aerial roots. There are only two species in the *Campsis* genus—the other is Chinese trumpet vine (*C. grandiflora*), a native of East Asia.

FAMILY: Bignoniaceae (bignonia family)

NATIVE RANGE: Central and North Florida

LIFESPAN: Perennial

BLOOM SEASON: Year-round, with peak bloom in late spring and summer

GROWTH HABIT: 30'+ long

PROPAGATION: Cuttings, division, seed

PLANTING: Plants are available in 1- and 3-gallon pot sizes. Find a place where plenty of sun exposure will produce many blooms. If placed on a trellis or fence, space plants about 3 feet apart. A freestanding, open-canopy tree, such as a pine that will permit plenty of filtered sunlight, also can be used.

CARE: Although Trumpet creeper does not need special care, it may need to be cut back frequently or trimmed to shape if it is confined to a specific area.

SITE CONDITIONS: Full sun to partial shade; moist sandy, loamy, or clay soils

HARDINESS: Zones 8A–9B

GARDEN TIPS: Because of its fast growth rate and potential size, Trumpet creeper may be difficult to control in a small setting. It is best used in a naturalistic landscape or, with persistent pruning, trained on a fence or large trellis. Do not let this plant grow on a house or other structure, as its aerial roots can damage wood, brick, stone, and stucco. It is deciduous in the north, while generally evergreen in the south.

KEITH BRADLEY

CAROLINA JESSAMINE
(Gelsemium sempervirens)

20 ft.

Carolina jessamine is an evergreen, woody, climbing or trailing vine that occurs naturally in mesic and hydric hammocks, pine flatwoods, thickets, bottomland swamps, and ruderal areas. It sometimes grows as an open trailing groundcover in the woods and also creates cascades of brilliant yellow as it grows up into trees and trails off branches. Its fragrant flowers typically bloom from winter through spring and will attract hummingbirds, butterflies, and large bees who will wriggle their way inside its tubular flowers.

Carolina jessamine flowers are lemon yellow and tubular with rounded, five-lobed calyces. They may be solitary or clustered. The plant's dark green glossy leaves are petiolate and elliptic to lanceolate with pointed tips. They are oppositely arranged. Leaf margins are entire. Seeds are flat with thin wings and are born in two-parted capsules.

FAMILY: Gelsemiaceae (gelsemium family)

NATIVE RANGE: Panhandle, north and central peninsula, Martin and Palm Beach counties

LIFESPAN: Perennial

BLOOM SEASON: Winter and spring

GROWTH HABIT: 20'+ long in multiple directions

PROPAGATION: Division (transplanting of suckers), cuttings, seed

PLANTING: Plants are available in 1- and 3-gallon containers. Space up to 3 feet apart for a groundcover or 2 feet apart for covering a fence. Water only to establish.

CARE: Carolina jessamine is generally pest free. It grows moderately fast but can be contained or shaped with pruning.

It may sucker and spread if allowed to run under mulch.

SITE CONDITIONS: Full sun to moderate shade; dry to moderately moist, well-drained soils

HARDINESS: Zones 8A–10B

GARDEN TIPS: Carolina jessamine is a great plant for winter color and is one of the first flowers to emerge in Florida in early January. This easy-to-grow vine adapts well to fences and trellises, where its small leaves and twining stems create an airy, light appearance. It also can be used as a groundcover or be allowed to climb trees, where it will flower in the canopy.

CAUTION: All parts of this plant are poisonous if swallowed. Do not plant in areas frequented by children or pets.

CORAL HONEYSUCKLE
(Lonicera sempervirens)

15 ft.

Coral honeysuckle is a robust, twining, woody vine that is mostly evergreen in Florida. The plant occurs naturally in sandhills, scrubby flatwoods, hardwood hammocks, flood-plain forests, and open woodlands. It blooms throughout the year in Central Florida, with best blooming in winter. Farther north, it has a reduced bloom season. The flowers are attractive to many butterflies, and hummingbirds find them irresistible. Birds enjoy the fruits.

Coral honeysuckle's showy tubular blooms are scarlet red to reddish orange with yellowish-orange throats. They grow to 2 inches or more in length and are born in dangling clusters. Stamens extend beyond the flower tube. Anthers are bright yellow. Leaves are oval to oblong with entire margins, dark green upper surfaces, and silvery-green undersides. They are oppositely arranged. Leaf attachment is sessile; however, those growing directly under or closest to the flower base are usually fully clasping the stem. Fruits are small, bright red berries.

FAMILY: Caprifoliaceae (honeysuckle family)

NATIVE RANGE: Panhandle, north and central peninsula

LIFESPAN: Perennial

BLOOM SEASON: Year-round in Central Florida; spring and summer in North Florida

GROWTH HABIT: 15'+ long

PROPAGATION: Air layering, cuttings, seed. Collect fruits when they are bright red, then remove, clean, and dry the seeds.

PLANTING: Plants are available in 1- and 3-gallon containers. Plant 2 feet apart along structures where it may climb or as a groundcover. Light shade will keep it more robust.

CARE: Occasional pruning of dead branches will keep it looking healthy.

SITE CONDITIONS: Full sun to moderate shade; dry to moist, well-drained acidic to slightly alkaline soils

HARDINESS: Zones 8A–10B

GARDEN TIPS: Coral honeysuckle is best if trained to a structure such as a fence, trellis, or arbor. Without a structure, it may develop only into a weak shrub. It can also be used as a groundcover in areas that are not used for walking. Combine with Yellow jessamine (*Gelsemium sempervirens*) for added interest.

NOTE: Unlike its invasive cousin, Japanese honeysuckle (*L. japonica*), Coral honeysuckle is not aggressive. Japanese honeysuckle can be distinguished from Coral honeysuckle by its yellow or white flowers.

PASSIONFLOWER
(Passiflora incarnata)

3–12 ft.

Purple passionflower, also known as Maypop, is an herbaceous, perennial vine that occurs naturally in Florida's open hammocks, along roadsides, and in disturbed areas. It is a larval host plant of several butterflies, including Gulf fritillary (exclusively), Variegated fritillary, and Zebra longwing. Bees, especially bumble and carpenter, find the flowers attractive and are the plant's primary pollinators.

Purple passionflower (pictured, top) has an extraordinarily intricate flower, resembling something out of a Dr. Seuss book. It has 10 lavender tepals, a purple and white fringed corona, a central "crown" of pink filaments, and conspicuous styles and stamens. The leaves are deeply three-lobed and alternately arranged, with dark green upper and whitish lower surfaces. The fruit is a large yellow-orange berry with edible pulp that is typically born in late summer to fall. The plant can be prostrate or climbing by way of axillary tendrils.

The fruit can be eaten raw or made into jam, jelly, or juice.

FAMILY: Passifloraceae (passionflower family)

NATIVE RANGE: Nearly throughout Florida

LIFESPAN: Perennial

BLOOM SEASON: Spring and summer

GROWTH HABIT: 3–12'+ long

PROPAGATION: Cutting, division, seed

PLANTING: Place this species along a fence, trellis, or other support where it can climb. It will spread above and underground, so site with caution.

CARE: Purple passionflower is easy to establish but harder to control. Competition from other plants and physical barriers help.

SITE CONDITIONS: Full sun to partial shade; dry to moist well-drained sandy, loamy, or calcareous soils

HARDINESS: Zones 8A–10B

GARDEN TIPS: Purple passionflower can spread vigorously on its own, covering a lot of ground in a short time. It is deciduous and will usually die back in the winter, and it is drought tolerant and moderately salt tolerant.

OTHER SPECIES: Corkystem passionflower (*P. suberosa*) (pictured, bottom) is found in moist hammocks and pinelands, coastal strands, and pine rocklands in peninsular Florida and into the Keys. Its flowers have no petals; five greenish-white sepals and a purple ring surround the stamen and pistil. Berries are green and turn bluish black when ripe. Both its flowers and fruits are much smaller than those of Purple passionflower. Corkystem passionflower gets its common name from the corky winglike structures that occur on older stems. This is a good option when the more vigorously spreading Purple passionflower is not desirable.

CAUTION: Tropical passionfruit (*Passiflora edulis*) is widely cultivated for its juice and is used to flavor fruit punches. It looks somewhat similar to Purple passionflower and has become naturalized in South Florida. *P. foetida* and *P. biflora* (an invasive species) also are becoming locally established and should be avoided.

TOP: RYAN FESSENDEN, BOTTOM: RYAN FESSENDEN

Grasses

NATIVE GRASSES GIVE TEXTURE and movement to a landscape—even a gentle breeze will cause them to sway and flow in graceful gestures. They are resilient, versatile, and have an understated beauty that adds elegance to any landscape. They also provide valuable resources to wildlife. Bunchgrasses, in particular, provide excellent cover and nesting habitat for birds, which also feast on seeds and the insects that subsist on the grass. Use native grasses as specimen plants or to fill open areas around other perennials. Intersperse bunchgrasses with tall wildflowers to help support them and keep them erect, or plant bunchgrasses of the same species en masse for greater impact.

BLUESTEM

(Andropogon ternarius, A. virginicus var. glaucus)

3–6 ft.

Bluestems are robust clump-forming grasses found primarily in pineland, sandhill, and scrub habitats throughout Florida. Many species occur in Florida, and their nomenclature continues to change. Splitbeard bluestem (*Andropogon ternarius*) and Chalky bluestem (*A. virginicus* var. *glaucus*, recently renamed *A. capillipes*) are two that are easily incorporated into landscapes. Bluestems offer cover, and the seeds provide food for a variety of birds and small animals.

Bluestem flowers are born in terminal racemes that vary in color from gold to white to silver, depending on the species, and are generally covered in soft hairs. Leaves are long and narrow with flattened leaf sheaths. The leaves of Splitbeard bluestem are flat, green on the upper surface and blue underneath. Chalky bluestem (pictured) leaves are covered in a chalky white coating, giving the plant a bluish or silvery color. Bluestems are bunchgrasses, meaning the leaves are born in tight clusters.

The genus name *Andropogon* is from the Greek *andro*, or "male," and *pogon*, or "beard," and refers to the bearded appearance of the inflorescence. Bluestems are sometimes known as "bearded grasses."

FAMILY: Poaceae (grass family)

NATIVE RANGE: Nearly throughout Florida

LIFESPAN: Perennial

BLOOM SEASON: Late summer and fall

GROWTH HABIT: 1–1½' tall and 1–2' wide; 3–6' tall when in bloom

PROPAGATION: Division, seed

PLANTING: Plants are available in liners or 1-gallon pots. Space them about 18 inches apart or mixed with wildflowers.

CARE: Allow spent flowering stems to remain through winter to provide interest in the garden as well as seeds for small birds. Cut back in spring before new growth emerges.

SITE CONDITIONS: Full sun to partial shade; dry to moist, well-drained sandy soils

HARDINESS: Zones 8A–10B

GARDEN TIPS: When used in a mixed planting with brightly colored wildflowers, bluestem grasses can provide a dramatic contrast. They also work well as accent plants or in masses.

NOTE: Some bluestems, such as Bushy bluestem (*A. glomeratus*), often are seen in ditches and wet disturbed areas, and Broomsedge bluestem (*A. virginicus* var. *virginicus*) is found in almost any disturbed spot. They will readily reseed if permitted and are not recommended for gardens.

MARY KEIM

WIREGRASS
(Aristida stricta)

1–3 ft.

Wiregrass is a perennial bunchgrass found in scrub, pine-lands, and coastal uplands throughout much of Florida. It is the dominant groundcover species in longleaf pine savannas and is a primary food source for gopher tortoises. Birds and small wildlife eat the seeds. Historically, cattle grazed on Wiregrass's tender new growth.

Wiregrass flowers are tiny and brown. They are born on spikelike terminal panicles. Flower stalks are elongated and extend above the leaves. Leaf blades are long, thin, and rolled inward, giving them a wiry appearance (hence the common name). They are erect and green when young and begin to arch and turn brown as they age. The fruits are small, yellowish caryopses. Seeds may be dispersed by wind, gravity, or on the fur of passing animals.

The genus name *Aristida* is from the Latin *arista*, meaning "awn," and refers to the three awns or bristlelike structures that extend from the florets. The species epithet *stricta* is from the Latin *strictus*, meaning "straight" or "erect."

FAMILY: Poaceae (grass family)

NATIVE RANGE: Nearly throughout Florida

LIFESPAN: Perennial

BLOOM SEASON: Spring through fall

GROWTH HABIT: 1–3'+ tall and equally wide

PROPAGATION: Division of bunches, seed. Germinate in winter or spring. Keep soil surface moist for several weeks.

PLANTING: Tubeling plugs and 1-gallon containers are available. Space 18 to 24 inches apart.

CARE: New leaf growth can be stimulated by cutting back old or dead foliage.

SITE CONDITIONS: Full sun to partial shade; very dry to moist, well-drained sandy soils

HARDINESS: Zones 8A–10B

GARDEN TIPS: Wiregrass is tolerant of drought conditions and low-nutrient soils. It is best suited for naturalistic landscapes and uplands restoration projects; however, individual specimens can be easily incorporated into a home wildflower garden. The plant is fire dependent, meaning it requires regular exposure to fire to stimulate flower and seed production.

HECTOR PEREZ

ELLIOTT'S LOVEGRASS
(Eragrostis elliottii)

1–2 ft.

Elliott's lovegrass is a perennial bunchgrass that occurs naturally in flatwoods, scrub, prairies, pond and wetland edges, and disturbed sites throughout Florida. Its delicate little flowers appear in such abundance that they cover the plant in a billowy beige haze. It typically blooms in late summer through fall. Its seeds are also tiny yet prolific, providing plenty of food for invertebrates and small birds, which also use the plant's dense foliage for cover. The plant is a larval host for the Zabulon skipper.

Elliott's lovegrass flowers are small, whitish beige, and born in wispy panicles. Leaves are long, linear, and erect or arching with a silvery or bluish hue. Its fruits are dry, one-seeded caryopses, typical of grasses. Seeds may be dispersed by wind and gravity or on the fur of passing animals.

The genus name *Eragrostis* comes from the Greek *eros*, or "love," and *agrostis*, meaning "grass." The species epithet *elliottii* and common descriptor "Elliott's" honors American botanist Stephen Elliott (1771–1830).

FAMILY: Poaceae (Gramineae) (grass family)

NATIVE RANGE: Throughout Florida

LIFESPAN: Perennial

BLOOM SEASON: Fall

GROWTH HABIT: 1–2' tall with a broader spread

PROPAGATION: Plants may be divided. Seeds germinate easily.

PLANTING: Available as tubelings or in 1-gallon containers. Plant in masses, mixed with wildflowers, or as a ground-cover.

CARE: Panicles will loosen when mature and tumble over the landscape, spreading seed. Gather seedheads before they ripen to control unwanted spread.

SITE CONDITIONS: Full sun; dry to moist, well-drained sandy soils

HARDINESS: Zones 8A–11A

GARDEN TIPS: Elliott's lovegrass can tolerate a variety of conditions. It does well in nutrient-poor soils, is drought tolerant, and can handle limited inundation. Its foliage remains attractive all year. The plant also is helpful in controlling erosion.

CAUTION: A South African cultivar, Wind dancer lovegrass, is often sold, as is the nonnative Weeping lovegrass (*E. curvula*), also from South Africa. Be sure you are purchasing the native species by sourcing from local growers.

NANCY BISSETT

MUHLYGRASS
(Muhlenbergia capillaris)

2–3 ft.

Muhlygrass is a robust, perennial, clump-forming grass that puts on a stunning fall display. It occurs naturally in coastal hammocks, strands, and grasslands; beach dunes; sandhills; and pine flatwoods. Its clumping habit provides excellent cover for wildlife.

Its flowers are pink to purplish red and tiny but profuse. They are born in long (1 to 2 feet), delicate panicles. Leaves are mostly basal and may reach 2 feet or more in length. Leaf blades are flat and thin but roll inward and become narrower toward the leaf tip. Stems are thin and glabrous. The fruit is a tiny caryopsis.

The genus name *Muhlenbergia* honors German-American amateur botanist Gotthilf Heinrich Ernst Muhlenberg (1753–1815). The species epithet *capillaris* is from the Latin *capillus*, or "hair," and *aris*, which means "of or pertaining to." It may refer to the fine, hairlike appearance of the inflorescence or the capillary- or tube-like form of the panicle branches or leaves.

FAMILY: Poaceae (grass family)

NATIVE RANGE: Nearly throughout Florida

LIFESPAN: Perennial

BLOOM SEASON: Fall

GROWTH HABIT: 2–3' tall and equally wide; taller when in bloom

PROPAGATION: Seed. Collect when the inflorescence has lost its purplish hue. Seed germinates readily.

PLANTING: Plants are generally available in 1- and 3-gallon containers. When planting in masses, space 3 feet apart.

CARE: Though not usually necessary, grasses may be cut back near the ground to encourage new spring growth. Spent bloom stalks may be trimmed.

SITE CONDITIONS: Full sun to partial shade; dry to moist, mildly acidic to alkaline sandy soils

HARDINESS: Zones 8A–11A

GARDEN TIPS: Muhlygrass is an excellent plant for most Florida landscapes. Its foliage is attractive all year, and its fall display of color is nothing short of spectacular. En masse, it produces a purplish-pink haze. It also is beautiful as a specimen plant. Muhlygrass is hardy, drought tolerant, and mildly salt and wind tolerant. It self-seeds and can maintain its population for many years. It also can serve as background for fall's blazing stars or Rayless sunflower.

KEVIN MAIN

LOPSIDED INDIANGRASS
(Sorghastrum secundum)

6 ft.

Lopsided indiangrass is a robust and unique perennial bunchgrass. It occurs naturally in pinelands, sandhills, and flatwoods. It typically blooms in late summer and fall. It is the larval host plant for the Delaware skipper, Dusted skipper, and Swarthy skipper.

Throughout most of the year, Lopsided indiangrass is rather indistinct. But in late summer, it produces tall, dramatic flower spikes. Each tiny flower is wrapped in bracts that are covered in soft bronze to brown hairs, and bears a long, twisted, reddish-brown awn and bright yellow anthers. When lit by the sun, the colorful flowerheads flicker and flash. The entire inflorescence occurs on one side of the rachis, hence the common descriptor "lopsided." Leaves are dark green with long-tapering blades up to 18 inches long.

The genus name *Sorghastrum* literally translates to "poor imitation of Sorghum." It is a combination of the genus *Sorghum* and the Latin suffix-*astrum*, meaning "expressing incomplete resemblance." The species epithet *secundum* is from the Latin *secundus*, meaning "following," "next," or (loosely) "in a row" and refers to the formation of flowers on one side of the rachis.

FAMILY: Poaceae (grass family)

NATIVE RANGE: Mostly throughout Florida

LIFESPAN: Perennial

BLOOM SEASON: Late summer and fall

GROWTH HABIT: 1½–2' tall; up to 6' when flowering

PROPAGATION: Clumps may be divided. Seed drops quickly after the flowerhead matures. Sow and lightly cover. Moisture causes the awns to twist and turn, which helps them burrow into the soil.

PLANTING: Plants are available in 1-gallon and smaller containers. Space about 2 feet apart.

CARE: Plants bloom the second year after seeding or exposure to fire. In large plantings, they can be mowed to about 8 inches; however, cutting them back to the ground may kill the plant. Old bloom stalks may be cut back.

SITE CONDITIONS: Full sun to minimal shade; dry to moist, well-drained soils

HARDINESS: Zones 8A–11A

GARDEN TIPS: Despite its height, Lopsided indiangrass does not generally obscure other plants. It makes a beautiful addition to naturalistic landscapes, wildflower gardens, or mixed meadows with other bunchgrasses and wildflowers. It also can be planted in small masses. Consider locating the plants where the sun will backlight the flowering stems.

FAKAHATCHEEGRASS
(Tripsacum dactyloides)

6 ft.

Also known as Eastern gamagrass, Fakahatcheegrass is a semi-showy bunchgrass that occurs naturally in hammocks, swamps, and wet ditches and along riverbanks throughout Florida. Although the flower is not especially striking, this robust plant can have a commanding presence in the landscape. Small wildlife and birds use it for cover. Birds and deer eat the seeds. Fakahatcheegrass is the larval host for the Clouded skipper and Three-spotted skipper.

The terminal inflorescence is composed of two or three spikes, with each spike containing both male and female spikelets. Male spikelets occur in pairs along the upper flower spike and have noticeable orange anthers. Female spikelets occur along the lower spike; stigmas are tufted and pale pinkish purple. All spikelets are sessile. Overall, the inflorescence appears brownish. Leaves are long (2 to 3 feet), narrow (about 1 inch wide), and flat with a conspicuous whitish midvein. The leaves tend to arch outward. Seeds are formed in stacked caryopses, which break off in segments.

FAMILY: Poaceae (grass family)

NATIVE RANGE: Throughout Florida

LIFESPAN: Perennial

BLOOM SEASON: Spring through fall

GROWTH HABIT: 3–4'+ tall (up to 6' when blooming) with 3–4'+ spread

PROPAGATION: Division, seed

PLANTING: Plants are readily available in quart, 1-, and 3-gallon containers. Space 3 to 4 feet apart in masses in moist soils.

CARE: Trim back dead portions as needed.

SITE CONDITIONS: Full sun to light shade; moist to wet, well- to poorly drained sandy or calcareous soils

HARDINESS: Zones 8A–10B

GARDEN TIPS: Fakahatcheegrass can add a note of strong texture to your landscape. It is well-suited for large landscapes where it can grow to its full potential, but a single accent plant may work as well in a small landscape. It also makes a nice border in areas with consistent moisture, and can help with soil stabilization when planted on a slope or along pond and stream edges. It tolerates infrequent but not lengthy inundation. It also may adapt to drier conditions, but is not drought tolerant. Fakahatcheegrass is clump-forming and spreads by self-sown seed. It may die back in the winter, particularly if temperatures dip below freezing.

OTHER SPECIES: Florida gamagrass (*Tripsacum floridanum*) occurs in the rocky pinelands of South Florida, is much smaller than Fakahatcheegrass, and is state-listed as endangered. It has folded rather than flat blades and a finer texture. Florida gamagrass can be easily used on drier sites and in masses or mixed with wildflowers. It too is readily available in 1- and 3-gallon containers.

Trees and Shrubs

TREES AND SHRUBS ARE ESSENTIAL COMPONENTS of a healthy, sustainable landscape. They host a variety of microhabitats, providing food and cover for myriad birds, small mammals, reptiles, amphibians, and insects. Shrubs can be a welcome addition as a privacy screen or buffer, while a tree can act as a centerpiece, giving your landscape a distinctive character. Many trees provide year-round interest with evergreen foliage or fall colors, vivid spring flowers, and abundant fruit. Shade trees can help lower electric bills by keeping your house cooler, particularly when planted on the east or west side of your home. Think carefully about the size, shape, and growth habit of trees and shrubs before planting to ensure they have the space they need to thrive.

RED MAPLE
(Acer rubrum)

30–50 ft.

Red maple is one of the most striking and common trees found in Florida's freshwater swamps and wetlands. For much of the year, its crown is covered in a scarlet hue—its flowers, fruits, and, for part of the year, leaves are all varying degrees of red. The tree provides food and cover for birds and other small wildlife. The foliage is food for many caterpillars, including the Rosy maple moth.

Red maple's showy but small flowers are red and born in hanging clusters in the leaf axils before new leaves emerge. Its distinctive leaves are simple, palmate, and three- to five-lobed with toothed margins. The upper leaf surface is green, while the underside is covered in whitish hairs, giving it a silvery tinge. Both the leaf stalk and veins are red. In the fall, when the first cold weather hits, the entire leaf turns red or reddish yellow. The trunk is generally straight with smooth gray bark. Seeds are born in two-winged samaras. The samara's papery coating allows the seed to be carried on the wind like a spinning helicopter, aiding in distribution far from the parent tree.

Red maple seeds are edible to humans but may be bitter. (Boiling them can lessen the bitterness.) Although maple syrup can be extracted from Red maple, it is not as plentiful or flavorful as that of its cousin Sugar maple (*Acer saccharum*).

FAMILY: Sapindaceae (soapberry family)

NATIVE RANGE: Nearly throughout Florida, except Hendry and Miami-Dade counties and the Keys

LIFESPAN: Perennial

BLOOM SEASON: Winter and early spring

GROWTH HABIT: 30'–50'+ tall

PROPAGATION: Seed

PLANTING: Plants are widely available in 1- to 200-gallon containers.

CARE: Red maple may produce many seedlings, but most do not mature and need not be weeded.

SITE CONDITIONS: Full sun to light shade; rich, moist to wet, well- to poorly drained soils

HARDINESS: Zones 8A–10B

GARDEN TIPS: Red maple is one of the first signs of spring, often flowering in January in Central Florida and gradually later to the north. Its attractive foliage and regular form make it a desirable specimen tree for moist or wet sites. Though a wetland plant, it can be used on moist sites or on drier, somewhat shady sites. The tree may be dioecious, meaning male and female flowers are born on separate plants, or monoecious, with male and female flowers on the same plant.

CAUTION: Many cultivars have been developed, but none are from Florida and are unlikely to perform well here.

MARLBERRY
(Ardisia escallonioides)

3–18 ft.

Marlberry is an evergreen shrub found in coastal strands and hammocks and pine rocklands throughout Central and South Florida. It blooms and fruits intermittently throughout the year, with peak blooming summer through fall. Marlberry's abundant fruit is enjoyed by birds and small animals and is also edible to humans. Its dense foliage provides significant cover for wildlife.

Marlberry's fragrant flowers may be creamy white or pinkish, have distinct yellow anthers, and are born in dense terminal or axillary panicles. The plant's thick, glossy, dark green leaves are lanceolate to elliptic and tend to reflex upward. They are petiolate and alternately arranged. Leaf margins are entire. Bark is smooth, thin, and whitish gray. Fruits begin as small green to reddish drupes that turn shiny and black when mature. Each fruit bears a single hard seed.

The genus name *Ardisia* is from the Greek *árdis*, or "point of an arrow," and may refer to the flowers' anthers or corolla lobes. The species epithet *escalloniodes* is derived from the genus *Escallonia* (named after the 18th century Spanish botanist Antonio Escallón y Flórez) and the Greek *eîdos*, meaning "resemblance" or "likeness."

FAMILY: Myrsinaceae (myrtle or eucalyptus family)

NATIVE RANGE: Peninsula from Flagler, Pasco, and Polk counties south into the Keys

LIFESPAN: Perennial

BLOOM SEASON: Year-round

GROWTH HABIT: 3–18'+ tall

PROPAGATION: Harvest seed from ripe fruit and sow in moist, shaded soils.

PLANTING: Available in 3-gallon and larger containers. Space 3 to 6 feet apart, depending on desired growth habit.

CARE: Marlberry is easy to trim to a preferred size and shape.

SITE CONDITIONS: Full sun to partial shade; moist, well-drained organic, sandy, or calcareous soils

HARDINESS: Zones 9A–11A

GARDEN TIPS: Marlberry is often overlooked as a landscape plant, but this shrub to small tree is attractive and versatile. It works well as a specimen plant, as a buffer, and in mass plantings.

CAUTION: Marlberry may be confused with its nonnative cousins, Coral ardisia (*Ardisia crenata*) and Shoebutton ardisia (*Ardisia elliptica*). Coral ardisia has crenately toothed leaf margins and red berries. Shoebutton ardisia's flowers are larger than Marlberry's and pinkish purple. Both are Category I invasives that are known to displace native species and alter natural communities. If present, they should be removed and destroyed.

GUMBO LIMBO
(Bursera simaruba)

30–50 ft.

Gumbo limbo is a large tree found in South Florida's tropical hammock habitats. It provides cover and food for birds and other small wildlife and is the larval plant for the Dingy purplewing butterfly. It also is known as the "tourist tree" for its peeling coppery-red bark that resembles the peeling skin of sunburnt tourists.

Gumbo limbo's inconspicuous five-petal flowers are greenish to yellowish white. Their prominent stamens are tipped by large, yellowish-orange anthers and are born in long terminal clusters. Leaves are pinnately compound, and leaflets are glossy and elliptic to ovate with entire margins. The trunk often is forked and twisted. Bark is thick, greenish brown, and resinous with a flaky, rust-colored outer layer. The crown is spreading and round. The fruit is a single-seeded capsule that is covered in a fleshy red seedcoat. The seedcoat is of particular interest to birds as it is high in lipids.

Native Americans used the resinous sap to trap songbirds.

The genus name *Bursera* is named after Danish botanist Joachim Burser (1583-1639).

FAMILY: Burseraceae (torchwood family)

NATIVE RANGE: Coastal counties from Volusia and Pinellas counties south into the Keys

LIFESPAN: Perennial

BLOOM SEASON: Winter and spring; may bloom year-round

GROWTH HABIT: 30–50' tall and as wide

PROPAGATION: Cuttings and even small branches will take root easily, but trees grown from seed may be hardier. Seeds germinate readily within a month.

PLANTING: Trees are available in 3- to 200-gallon containers and even larger field-grown sizes. Site this fast-growing tree where it can be appreciated for its bark and shade. Plant it alone or mixed with other trees, but leave enough room for it to spread.

CARE: Water well to establish. Once established, it should be free of maintenance.

SITE CONDITIONS: Full sun to light shade; moist, well-drained sandy or calcareous soils

HARDINESS: Zones 9B–11A

GARDEN TIPS: Gumbo limbo's spreading and often-twisted limbs and distinctive multicolored peeling bark make it an interesting choice as a specimen or shade tree. It is semi-deciduous, losing its leaves shortly before new leaves emerge. It is drought tolerant, hurricane resistant, and can withstand minimal amounts of saltwater inundation.

TAMARA ALVAREZ

AMERICAN BEAUTYBERRY
(Callicarpa americana)

3–6 ft.

Also known as French mulberry, American beautyberry is a woody shrub found in pinelands and hammocks throughout Florida. The plant's foliage offers cover for small wildlife. Its flowers are a nectar source for butterflies and bees, while its dense clusters of berries provide food for birds and deer from late summer into winter.

American beautyberry's small flowers may be pink, lavender, or white, emerging from leaf axils in late spring and early summer. Leaves are ovate to elliptic and petiolate with finely toothed margins, prominent pinnate venation, and a rough surface. They are oppositely arranged and are aromatic when crushed. Fruits are small (¼ to ½ inch in diameter) magenta drupes that are born in dense, conspicuous clusters along branches. Stems are square. Branches are loose and arching with grayish-brown bark.

The genus name *Callicarpa* is from the Greek *calli*, meaning "beauty," and *karpós*, meaning "fruit."

The fruits are edible to humans but have an astringent quality and not much flavor, making them somewhat unpalatable raw. Beautyberry jelly, however, is quite tasty. The leaves contain a chemical (callicarpenal) that may repel mosquitoes. Gently crush the leaf and rub it against the skin to release the chemical.

FAMILY: Lamiaceae (mint family)

NATIVE RANGE: Throughout Florida

LIFESPAN: Perennial

BLOOM SEASON: Late spring and early summer

GROWTH HABIT: 3–6' tall with up to 6' spread

PROPAGATION: Cuttings, seed. Depulped seed germinates easily, but seedling growth is slow.

PLANTING: Plants are readily available in 1- and 3-gallon containers. Plant about 4 or more feet apart to allow plants to gracefully arch their branches.

CARE: Allow plant to grow to its natural arching form. If desired, cut back in late winter for a denser form.

SITE CONDITIONS: Full sun to partial shade; dry to moist, well-drained sandy or calcareous soils

HARDINESS: Zones 8A–11A

GARDEN TIPS: American beautyberry is known for (and easily identified by) its prolific fruit production. It is adaptable to a variety of conditions but will flower and fruit more in full sun. The plant may become deciduous in North and north Central Florida.

AMERICAN HORNBEAM
(Carpinus caroliniana)

20–30 ft.

Also known as Musclewood and Blue beech, American hornbeam is a small handsome hardwood found in flood-plain forests in North and Central Florida. Its seeds and leaves provide food for birds and small wildlife, and it is the larval host for the Red-spotted purple, Tiger swallowtail, and Striped hairstreak butterflies.

American hornbeam's flowers are tiny, orangish yellow, and born in dangling catkins. Leaves are simple and oblong to ovate with doubly serrated margins. They are alternately arranged. New leaves are dark green but turn red, orange, or yellow in the fall. Its trunk is smooth and fluted, bearing resemblance to muscle. Its bark is dark bluish gray and smooth. The rounded crown is dense and typically symmetrical. Seeds are born in nutlets, each of which is surrounded by a three-winged bract that turns brown and papery when mature.

The genus name *Carpinus* is Latin for "hornbeam." The species epithet *caroliniana* is Latin for "from the Carolinas."

FAMILY: Betulaceae (birch family)

NATIVE RANGE: Panhandle, north and central peninsula

LIFESPAN: Perennial

BLOOM SEASON: Spring

GROWTH HABIT: 20–30'+ tall and as wide

PROPAGATION: Seed germination is improved with a cold stratification of two months.

PLANTING: Trees are generally available in 3-gallon containers. Plant in soil with some organic matter and keep well-watered until established. Consider siting where its distinctive trunk will be appreciated.

CARE: American hornbeam is deciduous, dropping its leaves before new ones emerge in spring. No special care is needed once well established. Its leaf litter provides useful organic material.

SITE CONDITIONS: Full sun to full shade; moist, well-drained sandy, clay, or loamy enriched soils

HARDINESS: Zones 8A–9B

GARDEN TIPS: Because of its small size, American hornbeam is a very usable tree in home landscapes, where it makes a nice specimen tree, particularly when its unique trunk can have the spotlight. It also can be used as an understory tree; however, planting in full sun will result in a denser crown.

BUTTONBUSH
(Cephalanthus occidentalis)

5–20 ft.

Buttonbush is a large, long-lived shrub that occurs naturally in wetlands and along stream and river edges. The flowers attract many bees, butterflies, and moths. Its seeds are eaten by ducks and other birds, and the foliage is browsed by deer.

The plant produces many globular white flowers with protruding pistils that give them a pincushion-like appearance. The fragrant flowers are about 2 inches in diameter. Buttonbush's leaves are dark green, elliptic to ovate, and shiny on top with pale undersides. They are up to 7 inches long and arranged in opposite pairs or in whorls. The plant is deciduous, losing its leaves in the winter with new ones emerging early in spring. Seeds are born in the fall in hard, reddish-brown, ball-like achenes.

The genus name *Cephalanthus* is from the Greek *kephalé*, or "head," and *ánthos*, or "flower." The species epithet *occidentalis* is Latin for "west" or "western," suggesting the plant is native to the western hemisphere.

FAMILY: Rubiaceae (coffee, bedstraw, or madder family)

NATIVE RANGE: Nearly throughout Florida

LIFESPAN: Perennial

BLOOM SEASON: Spring and summer

GROWTH HABIT: 5–20' tall

PROPAGATION: Soft-wood cuttings root easily. Seeds can be gathered in late summer or early fall and will germinate without any treatment.

PLANTING: Space large specimens 4 to 6 feet apart. Add some organic material to aid growth.

CARE: In shade, the foliage will be more open. Plants can be pruned to encourage denser foliage.

SITE CONDITIONS: Full sun to shade; wet sandy, clay, loamy, or mucky soils

HARDINESS: Zones 8A–11A

GARDEN TIPS: Because Buttonbush requires wet soil and its roots can withstand full submersion, it makes a great addition to pond and lake edges and wetland depressions.

CAUTION: The foliage is toxic to both humans and livestock.

EASTERN REDBUD
(Cercis canadensis)

15–30 ft.

Eastern redbud is a deciduous, perennial, large shrub to small tree. It occurs naturally in mesic hardwood hammocks and typically blooms in March, at which time the entire crown of the tree will become covered in deep pink blooms. Its leaves provide food for many caterpillars, including the Io moth. Flowers depend on long-tongued bees for pollination. The plant is browsed by white-tailed deer, and seeds are eaten by bobwhites and other birds.

Eastern redbud's irregular flowers are pink to magenta and born in clusters of four to eight within leaf axils and along branches and trunk. Flower buds are small, dark red to reddish brown, and appear in winter. They bloom in profusion before new leaves emerge. Young leaves are yellowish green and emerge folded along the midrib. As they mature, they unfurl and turn a dull green. They are paper-thin and cordate to orbicular with entire margins and a pointed apex. Arrangement is alternate. In the fall, they may turn bright yellow. The trunk is often twisted and covered in gray to reddish-brown bark. Branches are thin and may zigzag as they grow. Fruits are flattened pods that contain 10 seeds or more.

Both flowers and seeds are edible. Flowers can be eaten raw or boiled, and seeds may be roasted.

FAMILY: Fabaceae (legume, bean, or pea family)

NATIVE RANGE: Panhandle; north and west central peninsula

LIFESPAN: Perennial

BLOOM SEASON: Spring

GROWTH HABIT: 15–30' tall with crown spreading to 10–30'

PROPAGATION: Seeds have a hard, impermeable coat. To crack open, place seeds in a cup, pour boiling water on them, and let them stand for 24 hours. It may be necessary to follow this with a cold moist stratification by placing seeds in a refrigerator for five weeks or more.

PLANTING: Trees are available in 3- to 30-gallon containers. Because of their wide spread, plant 10 or more feet apart.

CARE: Redbud is susceptible to canker, so diseased branches should be pruned as soon as they are noticed. The brown pods can be removed if neatness is desired, as they will persist into winter, but remember that birds eat the seeds.

SITE CONDITIONS: Full sun to partial shade; moist, well-drained, neutral to mildly acidic soils

HARDINESS: Zones 8A–9B

GARDEN TIPS: Redbud is a relatively fast-growing flowering tree. It can tolerate occasional periods of brief flooding. Plant it with Flowering dogwood for a beautiful, colorful spring display.

CAUTION: Many cultivars of Eastern redbud have been developed. Select trees grown from local seed sources for best results.

KATHERINE EDISON

SNOWBERRY
(Chiococca alba)

6–10 ft.

Snowberry is a robust, evergreen, vine-like shrub that occurs naturally in pine rocklands, shell mounds, and coastal strands and hammocks. Its fragrant flowers typically bloom spring through fall but may bloom year-round. Its showy white fruits also are usually present. This plant is a larval host for the endangered Miami blue butterfly and Snowberry clearwing moth. Its flowers provide nectar for Julia butterflies and a variety of other insects, and its berries are consumed by birds and other wildlife.

Snowberry's yellow to creamy-white flowers are small (up to ½ inch), five-lobed, and bell-shaped. They are born in panicles. Leaves are dark green with entire margins and are oppositely arranged. They may be elliptic, ovate, or broadly lanceolate. Stems are angled and woody. Branches are slim and vine-like. Fruits are white, round or oblong drupes.

The genus name *Chiococca* comes from the Greek *chion*, meaning "snow," and *kokkos*, meaning "kernel" or "berry." The species epithet *alba* is Latin for "white." Both names refer to the color of its berries.

FAMILY: Rubiaceae (coffee, bedstraw, or madder family)

NATIVE RANGE: Most coastal peninsular counties

LIFESPAN: Perennial

BLOOM SEASON: Spring through fall; sometimes year-round

GROWTH HABIT: 6–10' tall and equally wide

PROPAGATION: Clean seeds of fruit flesh, cover lightly with soil, and keep moist.

PLANTING: Available in 1- and 3-gallon containers. Plant in light shade with enough room to sprawl.

CARE: Snowberry sprawls and climbs over other vegetation, so it may require trimming to keep it in check.

SITE CONDITIONS: Partial shade; dry to moderately moist, well-drained sandy or calcareous soils

HARDINESS: Zones 9A–11A

GARDEN TIPS: Snowberry's habit varies between shrub and vine. It can be aggressive in the garden so is better suited for naturalistic or restoration landscapes; however, it also works well as a buffer plant. It tolerates salt and drought.

RYAN FESSENDEN

COCOPLUM
(Chrysobalanus icaco)

3–15 ft.

Cocoplum is an evergreen shrub or small tree native to swamps, coastal dunes, and hammocks in Central and South Florida. It produces flowers and fruits throughout the year, with the peak bloom occurring winter through spring. Its dense foliage and substantial fruit provide cover and food for many birds and small wildlife. Flowers attract pollinators, especially bees.

Cocoplum's inconspicuous flowers are white to greenish white and born in clusters at the leaf base. Leaves are leathery, broadly ovate to round, and up to 3 inches long. They have a pointy tip and a short petiole and are bright green, often with a reddish tint. They are alternately arranged but tend to grow upward, appearing as if they are growing on the same side of the stem. Fruits are drupes that vary in color from white to pinkish to dark purple. Each contains a single seed encased in a stone. The trunk is multibranched with brown or reddish-brown bark.

The flesh of Cocoplum fruit can be eaten raw or made into a tasty jam. The oil-rich seed (once removed from its hard stone) can be eaten raw or cooked.

FAMILY: Chrysobalanaceae (cocoplum family)

NATIVE RANGE: Coastal counties from Brevard and Sarasota south, Pasco County, and the Keys

LIFESPAN: Perennial

BLOOM SEASON: Year-round

GROWTH HABIT: 3–15'+ tall and equally wide

PROPAGATION: Cleaned seeds germinate slowly and may not be true to type. Air-layering and cuttings are most effective in preserving varieties.

PLANTING: Plants are available in 1- to 7-gallon containers. Plant 3 or more feet apart, depending on purpose.

CARE: Prune only if necessary to keep a desired size or shape.

SITE CONDITIONS: Full sun to partial shade; moist to wet, well- to poorly drained sandy, calcareous, or organic soils

HARDINESS: Zones 9B–11A

GARDEN TIPS: Cocoplum produces more fruit and denser vegetation when planted in full sun. It is an excellent choice for hedge or buffer plantings and also works well as a specimen or accent shrub. The plant adapts well to a variety of landscape conditions and is tolerant of drought and high winds.

NOTE: Both spreading and erect forms of Cocoplum exist. The coastal-growing Horizontal variety is low growing, spreading, and salt tolerant. Its creeping branches root where they touch the ground, so it is a good plant for dune stabilization and to help prevent erosion. The inland-growing Red tip and Green tip varieties have more-upright forms and are not salt tolerant. All varieties can hybridize when grown in close proximity to another variety. Be sure to choose the variety and form best suited to your landscape. .

LEA KINDT

PIGEON PLUM
(Coccoloba diversifolia)

30–40 ft.

Pigeon plum is an attractive small tree native to South Florida's coastal hammocks. Its flowers provide nectar for a variety of butterflies, and its fruits are eaten by birds and other small animals. They also are edible to humans. Though tart, they can be made into a good jelly.

Pigeon plum's flowers are tiny with greenish-white petals and sepals. They are born on long, compact spikes. Leaves are leathery, oblong to oval, and can vary in length from 2 to 12 inches. They are alternately arranged. Leaf margins are entire and undulating to revolute. The crown is densely branched. Bark is gray, but it become mottled and flaky as the tree matures. Fruits are green berrylike achenes that turn reddish purple and juicy when ripe.

The genus name *Coccoloba* is from the Greek *kókkos*, or "berry," and *lobós*, meaning "lobe" or "pod." The species epithet *diversifolia* is from the Latin *diversus*, or "different," and *folius*, or "leaf," and refers to the variability of leaf size and shape.

FAMILY: Polygonaceae (buckwheat family)

NATIVE RANGE: South Florida from Lee County south, and east coast counties north to Brevard

LIFESPAN: Perennial

BLOOM SEASON: Spring and summer, but may bloom year-round

GROWTH HABIT: 30–40' tall; taller than wide

PROPAGATION: Clean seed and sow immediately.

PLANTING: Plants are available in 3- to 100-gallon containers and even larger field-grown trees. Select a site where the abundant fallen fruit will not be a problem. If plants are used in masses, space them 10 or more feet apart, depending on the goal. It is a moderate grower.

CARE: Pigeon plum does not generally have a problem with self-seeding. No other care is needed unless trimming to keep size in check is desired.

SITE CONDITIONS: Full sun to partial shade; moist, well-drained sandy or calcareous soils

HARDINESS: Zones 9B–11A

GARDEN TIPS: Pigeon plum's dense foliage and attractive bark make it ideal as a specimen tree or as a buffer or screen. It is especially good for coastal landscapes, as it can tolerate drought, salt, and hurricane winds. It is dioecious, which means both a male and female specimen are needed to ensure pollination and fruit.

BUTTONWOOD
(Conocarpus erectus)

20–40 ft.

Buttonwood is an evergreen small tree or shrub usually associated with the mangroves that it typically grows alongside. It is a significant host for many epiphytic plant species. The tree provides food and cover for wildlife, and its flowers provide nectar for some butterflies and moths. It also is a larval host plant for Martial hairstreak butterflies and Tantalus sphinx moths.

Buttonwood's pincushion-like inflorescence consists of many greenish, petal-less flowers that are born in globose panicles. Leaves are simple and oblong with entire margins and alternate arrangement. The upper surface is shiny, while the underside is covered in fine hairs. The trunk may be straight or gnarled if exposed to wind. The fruits are cone-shaped aggregates that turn purplish brown when mature.

The genus name *Conocarpus* is from the Latin *conicus*, which means "cone" or "cone-shaped," and the Greek word *karpós*, or "fruit." The species epithet *erectus* is Latin for "upright."

FAMILY: Combretaceae

NATIVE RANGE: Coastal counties from Volusia on the east coast and Levy on the west, south into the Keys

LIFESPAN: Perennial

BLOOM SEASON: Year-round, with peak bloom in summer

GROWTH HABIT: 20–40'+ tall and equally wide

PROPAGATION: Air-layering, cuttings, seed

PLANTING: Plants are available in 1- to 50-gallon containers and larger field-grown specimens. Water until established.

CARE: Buttonwood can be pruned into a desired shape when used as a screen or buffer. No special care is needed.

SITE CONDITIONS: Full sun; moderately dry, moist, or periodically inundated sandy or calcareous soils

HARDINESS: Zones 9A–11A

GARDEN TIPS: Buttonwood may not be the most eye-catching plant, but it is incredibly durable, tolerating drought, hurricane winds, and salt water at its roots during high tide. It also is resistant to most pests. It is well-suited to be an accent or specimen plant and will do well in a variety of soils. Unfortunately, Buttonwood is often kept very low as a clipped hedge, eventually resulting in thin foliage on stunted trunks. It is best maintained as a tree. It is generally dioecious, meaning male and female flowers are born on separate plants.

NOTE: Much of the buttonwood grown commercially is Silver buttonwood, which has striking silvery foliage. Generally smaller in size, it is used more frequently than Buttonwood. It is found in the Keys and along the lower southwest coast. Sometimes referred to as *Conocarpus erectus* var. *sericeus*, it is not accepted as a taxonomic variety since the hairiness that gives it a silvery sheen varies from plant to plant, much like the east coast's Silver palmetto. However, growers often select the silver form to propagate, and some cultivars even have been named for it.

FLOWERING DOGWOOD
(Cornus florida)

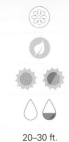

20–30 ft.

When in bloom, Flowering dogwood is arguably one of Florida's most beautiful flowering trees. Though dormant in winter, the tree comes alive in early spring. Before leaves emerge, a bounty of showy white to pinkish blooms cover the crown. From late summer to fall, its abundant fruit provides food for a variety of birds and small mammals. Flowering dogwood occurs naturally along the edges of mesic hardwood forests and pinelands throughout North and much of Central Florida.

On first sight, flowers appear to have four large white petals with greenish-yellow centers. In fact, those "petals" are bracts, and the centers are a cluster of tiny flowers, each with minute greenish-yellow bracts. The large bracts are typically white but may be pinkish to almost red. They are broadly ovate with a distinctly notched apex. Flowers are born in clusters on the tips of each branch. Leaves are simple and ovate with entire margins and veins that curve toward the apex. Leaf arrangement is opposite. Fruits are large, bright red drupes born in clusters of 2 to 10. The tree can be single- or multi-trunked. Branches spread in horizontal layers to give it a pleasing shape.

FAMILY: Cornaceae (dogwood family)

NATIVE RANGE: Panhandle, peninsula south to Orange, Polk, and Manatee counties (excluding most east coast counties)

LIFESPAN: Perennial

BLOOM SEASON: Spring

GROWTH HABIT: 20–30' tall with crown spreading to 15–20' wide

PROPAGATION: Cuttings, seed. Cuttings generally require a mist system to keep the plants moist. Dormant seed should be cold-stratified for three to four months before sowing.

PLANTING: An ideal setting for Florida dogwood is the understory of large oaks or other deciduous trees. Be sure to source locally, as plants from northern states do not bloom or do well in Florida.

CARE: Dogwoods are susceptible to an anthracnose fungus and dogwood borers. The best defense is to plant in settings that do not stress the tree.

SITE CONDITIONS: Full sun to partial shade; dry to moist, well-drained acidic soils

HARDINESS: Zones 8A–9B

GARDEN TIPS: In the right conditions, Flowering dogwood is easy to grow and relatively maintenance free. However, it does not tolerate alkaline soils or prolonged exposure to intense heat. If planting in full sun, additional irrigation may be necessary.

KEITH BRADLEY

BEACH CREEPER
(Ernodea littoralis)

1–2 ft.

Also known as Golden creeper and Coughbush, Beach creeper is an evergreen, low growing, mat-forming shrub found on dunes, beaches, coastal hammock edges, and pine rocklands throughout Central and South Florida. It produces flowers and fruits year-round. The nectar attracts butterflies and hummingbirds, while the berries provide food for birds and small wildlife.

The pink to pinkish-white flowers are sessile and axillary. Corollas are long (½ inch) and tubular with four recurved lobes. The glossy bright-green leaves are lanceolate to elliptic and fleshy with entire margins and bowed venation. They are oppositely arranged. Stems are woody and reddish with curving branches. Fruit is a round to oval golden-colored drupe containing a single seed.

The genus name *Ernodea* is from the Greek *ernos*, meaning "sprout" or "bud," alluding to the spreading nature of the plant. The species epithet *littoralis* is from the Latin *litoralis*, or "of the seashore."

FAMILY: Rubiaceae (coffee, madder, or bedstraw family)

NATIVE RANGE: Coastal counties from Volusia south to the Keys, and Pinellas and Hillsborough south to Monroe mainland

LIFESPAN: Perennial

BLOOM SEASON: Year-round

GROWTH HABIT: 1–2' tall and 3–6'+ wide and spreading

PROPAGATION: Seed; cuttings from tips may root easily.

PLANTING: Plants are available in 1- to 3-gallon containers. Plant 3 feet apart to account for a moderate growth rate.

CARE: Prune if needed to keep sprawling in check.

SITE CONDITIONS: Full sun to light shade; dry to moist, well-drained sandy or calcareous soils

HARDINESS: Zones 9A–11A

GARDEN TIPS: Beach creeper makes an interesting groundcover, especially in hot, dry areas where other plants may struggle to survive, such as rocky or gravelly areas and parking lots. The plant is drought tolerant and can persist for many years. It is also great for erosion control.

BEN KOLSTAD

CORALBEAN
(Erythrina herbacea)

Coralbean gets its common name from its coral-colored seeds. It is also known as Cardinal spear, which refers to its red tubular flowers. It is a deciduous to evergreen woody shrub found in coastal hammocks, sandhills, flatwoods, mesic and upland woods, and pine rocklands throughout Florida. Its striking scarlet flowers attract hummingbirds, bumblebees, and butterflies.

3–8 ft.

Coralbean's flowers are born in long (4 to 6+ inches) terminal racemes. Individual flowers may be as long as 3 inches. Leaves are compound and composed of three light green, deltoid-shaped leaflets, each with tiny prickles along the undersides of its margins. The stem and irregular branches also are armed with short curved spines. Bark is light gray to whitish and may be rough or smooth. Fruits are large, light, drooping pods that turn nearly black and split open when mature. Seeds are shiny and bright red with a black spot or stripe.

The genus name *Erythrina* is from the Greek *erythrós*, meaning "red."

FAMILY: Fabaceae (legume, bean, or pea family)

NATIVE RANGE: Nearly throughout Florida

LIFESPAN: Perennial

BLOOM SEASON: Winter and spring

GROWTH HABIT: 3–8' tall, but has been known to grow as tall as 20' in South Florida

PROPAGATION: Scarify seeds by nipping the seed coat before planting in spring.

PLANTING: Plants are available in 1- to 7-gallon and larger containers. Plant in small groups and space at least 3 feet apart.

CARE: Trim back old flowering stems and collect seed if desired. In North

Florida, plants may freeze to the ground. Although not common, *Erythrina* moths may use the plant as a host, resulting in dead stem tips.

SITE CONDITIONS: Full sun to partial shade; dry to moist, sandy or calcareous soils

HARDINESS: Zones 8A–11A

GARDEN TIPS: Coralbean is an incredibly versatile plant. It is drought tolerant, salt tolerant, and pest resistant, making it the perfect addition to many Florida landscapes. It is very showy when it blooms.

CAUTION: This plant contains toxic alkaloids that may result in paralysis if ingested. Keep it away from pets and small children. Gloves are recommended when working with seeds.

WHITE STOPPER
(Eugenia axillaris)

15 ft.

White stopper is an evergreen shrub or small tree found in coastal hammocks, strands, and shell mounds in Florida's central and southern peninsula. Its fragrant flowers bloom year-round, with peak blooming in spring and summer, attracting many types of pollinators. Fruits generally form in fall and may persist several months. They are eaten by birds and wildlife. Humans can eat them, too—the flesh is quite sweet when ripe, but eating the bitter seeds is not recommended.

White stopper's flowers are four-petaled with many obvious stamens, which give the flower a frilly appearance. They are born in axillary clusters. Leaves are elliptic to ovate, dark green on top and pale underneath, with entire margins and reddish petioles. Young leaves may be pinkish or red. Mature leaves may be studded with black dots. Leaf arrangement is opposite. White stopper's trunk is smooth with light grayish to whitish bark. Fruits are round, medium-sized fleshy berries about ½ inch in diameter. Immature fruits are green; mature fruit varies from red to purplish black.

The common name "stopper" alludes to the plant's historical use as a treatment for diarrhea.

FAMILY: Myrtaceae (myrtle or eucalyptus family)

NATIVE RANGE: Central and southern peninsula into the Keys

LIFESPAN: Perennial

BLOOM SEASON: Year-round

GROWTH HABIT: 15'+ tall

PROPAGATION: Harvest seeds when ripe; clean before sowing.

PLANTING: Plants are available in 1- to 25-gallon containers.

CARE: Requires little to no maintenance once established.

SITE CONDITIONS: Full sun to partial shade (ideal); moist, well-drained calcareous, loamy, or sandy soils

HARDINESS: Zones 9A–11A

GARDEN TIPS: White stopper is an attractive addition to a variety of landscapes. Its copious blooms are striking against its dark green leaves. The plant's dense foliage and ability to be pruned into any desired shape make it a good option for a hedge or buffer. Individual specimens are typically symmetrical and work well in formal settings.

SPANISH STOPPER
(Eugenia foetida)

8–15 ft.

Spanish stopper is an evergreen shrub or small tree native to coastal hardwood hammocks and thickets in Central and South Florida. Its semi-showy flowers bloom year-round, with peak blooming in spring and summer, attracting many types of pollinators. Its dense foliage provides cover, and its abundant fruit provides food for birds and other small animals.

Spanish stopper's four-petaled flowers are white with many obvious stamens, giving the flower a frilly appearance. They are born in axillary clusters. Leaves are simple, leathery, ovate, and dark green with yellowish undersides. The petioles are reddish. Leaf apices are rounded, visually separating the plant from other stoppers. Leaf margins are entire and appear yellow. Leaf arrangement is opposite. Crown is relatively narrow. Bark is smooth and brownish gray; it may be scaly in older specimens. Fruits are small (about ¼ inch in diameter), round, fleshy berries that are reddish in color, turning purplish black when mature.

The species epithet *foetida* is the female form of the Latin word *foetidus*, meaning "bad smelling." It refers to the foul smell emitted by the flowers and leaves, particularly in the summer. The common name "stopper" alludes to the plant's historical use as a treatment for diarrhea.

FAMILY: Myrtaceae (myrtle or eucalyptus family)

NATIVE RANGE: Coastal counties from Brevard and Manatee south to the Keys

LIFESPAN: Perennial

BLOOM SEASON: Year-round with peak bloom in summer

GROWTH HABIT: 8–15' tall

PROPAGATION: Seed. Harvest when ripe; clean before sowing.

PLANTING: Plants are available in 3- to 200-gallon containers and field grown. Space plants according to goal, as close as 3 feet for shorter plants to 5 or 6 feet apart. Ideally, plant in moist soil with a range of pH. Water well to establish.

CARE: Established plants will be tolerant of short drought periods, but water if needed. Trim as desired. Plants generally grow slowly.

SITE CONDITIONS: Full sun to partial shade (ideal); dry to moist, well-drained calcareous, loamy, or sandy soils with some organic material

HARDINESS: Zones 9B–11A

GARDEN TIPS: Spanish stopper's dense foliage and ability to be pruned into any desired shape make it a good option for a screen or buffer, as well as for an accent or specimen plant. Its slender form makes it especially suited for narrow spaces. It is moderately drought tolerant and can withstand hurricane and salt winds, making it ideal for coastal areas.

FLORIDA PRIVET
(Forestiera segregata)

8–15 ft.

Florida privet is an evergreen shrub to small tree that occurs naturally in coastal hammocks, thickets, scrub, and pine rocklands. Flowers typically appear in early spring before leaves emerge, but the plant may bloom year-round. Bees, flies, and butterflies are attracted to the flowers. Birds and small mammals use the dense foliage for cover and are partial to the abundant fruit that ripens in early summer when few fruits are available.

Florida privet's tiny flowers are greenish yellow and born in axillary clusters. Stamens are extended and bifurcated with orange or brown anthers. The plant's simple leaves are oblong to elliptic with blunt tips and entire margins. Undersides are finely punctate. Leaf arrangement is opposite. Bark is thin and grayish brown. Fruits are purple to blackish-blue olive-like berries that are about ½ inch long. Each berry contains a single seed.

The genus name *Forestiera* pays homage to the 18th century French botanist and physician André Robert Forestier.

FAMILY: Oleaceae (olive family)

NATIVE RANGE: Coastal peninsular counties from Duval and Dixie south to the Keys

LIFESPAN: Perennial

BLOOM SEASON: Spring; year-round in the south

GROWTH HABIT: 8–15' tall with 5–10' spread

PROPAGATION: Seed. Clean well before sowing.

PLANTING: Plants are available in 1- to 7-gallon containers. Space 4 to 5 feet apart for mass plantings.

CARE: Florida privet is relatively maintenance free once established.

SITE CONDITIONS: Full sun to partial shade; dry to moist, well-drained sandy, loamy, or calcareous soils

HARDINESS: Zones 8B–11A

GARDEN TIPS: Florida privet is an ideal plant for the shady edge of a garden. It works well in a buffer or hedge or as a specimen plant. The plant can be pruned to a desired height or shape. It is dioecious, which means both a male and female specimen are needed to ensure pollination and fruit. Florida privet is drought and salt tolerant. It is generally evergreen but may be briefly deciduous in northern climes.

GARBERIA
(Garberia heterophylla)

3–5 ft.

Garberia is unlike most species in the Asteraceae family in that its growth habit is woody and shrubby rather than herbaceous. Garberia is endemic to Florida's north and central peninsula, and occurs naturally in scrub and xeric hammocks. It typically flowers in late fall but has been known to flower sparsely throughout the year. It is a state-listed threatened species and is part of the Eupatorieae tribe, whose members produce flowers consisting of only disk and no ray florets. It is an excellent nectar source for many butterflies and bees.

Garberia's inflorescences are large, showy clusters of pink to purple flowers. Individual disk florets are tubular and have conspicuously extended styles. Ray florets are absent. Leaves are oval to obovate with undulating entire margins and a distinctly grayish-green hue. They are alternately arranged. Bark is also grayish in color. Seeds are born in tiny achenes.

The genus name *Garberia* honors American botanist Abraham Garber (1838–1881). The species epithet *heterophylla* is from the Greek *hetero*, which means "diverse," and *phúllon*, which means "leaf."

FAMILY: Asteraceae (aster, composite, or daisy family)

NATIVE RANGE: Clay and Putnam counties, Central Florida south to Highlands County

LIFESPAN: Perennial

BLOOM SEASON: Fall with peak bloom from late October to November

GROWTH HABIT: 3–5' tall with equal spread

PROPAGATION: Sow seed in winter and cover lightly.

PLANTING: Plants are available in 1-gallon containers. Space about 3 feet apart in sandy soil and water as needed until established.

CARE: Garberia does not require much maintenance once established. Be sure to not overwater or overfertilize.

SITE CONDITIONS: Full sun to minimal shade; dry, well-drained, sandy acidic soils

HARDINESS: Zones 8A–9B

GARDEN TIPS: Garberia works well in dry, sunny areas in a mixed shrub bed or as a single specimen. In normal conditions, it is evergreen and is particularly long-lived. It is drought tolerant and, once established, requires little to no irrigation.

FIREBUSH

(*Hamelia patens* var. *patens*)

10 ft.

Firebush is a hardy, fast-growing, showy evergreen shrub to small tree found in hardwood hammocks and coastal and upland forests. It typically blooms spring through fall but can bloom year-round in warmer climes. Its nectar-filled blooms vary in length, attracting both butterflies and hummingbirds. Its berries are plentiful and are eaten by a variety of birds and small mammals. They are also edible to humans, although the taste is not particularly desirable.

Firebush produces clusters of bright orange to red thinly tubular flowers. Leaves are elliptical to ovate with entire margins and pointed tips. Petioles and veins are often reddish. Leaf arrangement is usually whorled but may be opposite. Fruits are small green berries that turn red and then purplish black as they mature. They are born in clusters.

The genus name *Hamelia* honors the French botanist Henry Louis Hamel de Monceau (1700–1782). The species epithet *patens* is Latin for "spreading" or "to be open" and refers to the plant's growth habit.

FAMILY: Rubiaceae (coffee, bedstraw, or madder family)

NATIVE RANGE: Central and southern peninsula from Marion County south

LIFESPAN: Perennial

BLOOM SEASON: Spring through fall; year-round in South Florida

GROWTH HABIT: Up to 10' tall with 3–6'+ spread

PROPAGATION: Cuttings, seed. Clean seed before sowing.

PLANTING: Firebush is cold-sensitive and will die back in a freeze. Space plants 3 feet apart in freeze-prone areas; use wider spacing in warmer areas where plants will grow larger. Plant in full sun for best flowering or more shade for attractive foliage.

CARE: Firebush is relatively maintenance and pest free. It can self-seed, but seedlings can be easily moved or pulled. Trim only if needed, or cut back after a freeze.

SITE CONDITIONS: Full sun to full shade; dry to moist sandy, somewhat alkaline soils

HARDINESS: Zones 8B–11A

GARDEN TIPS: Firebush is one of Florida's best plants for attracting butterflies and birds. It can be used as a specimen plant or in a border or mass planting. It is relatively tolerant of salt and wind and is a moderately fast grower.

CAUTION: Avoid nonnative varieties of firebush, particularly *H. patens* var. *glabra* (frequently sold as African, Dwarf, or Compact firebush), as it may interbreed with the native firebush. Calusa firebush is a native cultivar that may be used if a more compact size is desirable.

ATLANTIC ST. JOHN'S WORT
(Hypericum tenuifolium)

1–1½ ft.

St. John's wort is an evergreen shrub known for its outstanding ornamental features. Thirty-four species are found in Florida. All are native, and several are on state and federal endangered plant lists. Atlantic St. John's wort is the most typical species encountered at native plant nurseries and plant sales. It occurs naturally in scrub, pine flatwoods, sandhills, and coastal swales. Its many golden flowers bloom in the summer, attracting a host of native bees and other pollinators.

Atlantic St. John's wort has small (less than 1 inch in diameter) bright yellow flowers with five petals, five sepals, and many obvious yellow-orange stamens. Leaves are dark green, needlelike, and typically less than ½ inch long. They are sessile and oppositely arranged. Stems are reddish brown and sturdy. Seeds are born in capsules. The shrub has a delightful mounding and spreading shape.

The species epithet *tenuifolium* is from the Latin *tenuis*, or "thin," and *folius*, or "leaf."

FAMILY: Hypericaceae (St. John's wort family)

NATIVE RANGE: Peninsula, central and western Panhandle

LIFESPAN: Perennial

BLOOM SEASON: Summer

GROWTH HABIT: 1–1½' tall with 2'+ spread

PROPAGATION: Collect seeds from plants when dry. Sow directly in the garden in the fall for spring growth.

PLANTING: Plants are available in 1-gallon containers. Space plants 24 to 36 inches apart. Without competition it can spread to 4 feet but will be smaller when near other plants.

CARE: This hardy perennial is easy to care for once established. It may need additional water during spring droughts.

SITE CONDITIONS: Full sun to partial shade; dry to moist, well-drained sandy soils

HARDINESS: Zones 8A–10B

GARDEN TIPS: Atlantic St. John's wort can be used as a foundation plant, along a border or edge, or in a mass planting. It can adapt to a variety of soils, including clay and loam, as well as acidic and lightly alkaline soils. Plants are not salt tolerant and are moderately drought tolerant once established.

CAUTION: The St. John's wort promoted as a supplement for use in treating depression is a nonnative species. According to Dan Austin in *Florida Ethnobotany*, using native St. John's wort can lead to dermatitis or photosensitization due to a hypericin compound found in the plants. Some species may be toxic to livestock.

MARY KEIM

DAHOON HOLLY
(Ilex cassine)

15–30 ft.

Dahoon holly is an evergreen tree or large shrub with exceptional landscape potential. It is easy to grow and attractive year-round. Its dense foliage and abundant fruit are attractive to birds and other small wildlife. It occurs naturally in swamps, seepage slopes, and hammocks and along pond edges.

Its small flowers have four or five yellowish-white petals surrounding a green superior ovary. They are born in showy axillary clusters. Leaves are simple, shiny, and oblong with entire margins and bristly apices. (Margins are sometimes finely serrated, especially toward the tip.) Leaf arrangement is alternate. Crown is generally irregular. Bark is gray and smooth; it may be scaly in older specimens and covered with lichens, mosses, or other epiphytes. Fruits are small, bright red drupes that are prolific from late fall through winter and occasionally into spring.

Dahoon holly with fruit is often used in Christmas decorations.

FAMILY: Aquifoliaceae (holly family)

NATIVE RANGE: Throughout Florida, except the Keys

LIFESPAN: Perennial

BLOOM SEASON: Late spring

GROWTH HABIT: 15–30' tall; taller than wide

PROPAGATION: Cuttings, seed. Unlike many other holly species, seeds germinate without special treatment.

PLANTING: Plants are available in 1- to 50-gallon pots and field grown. If planting masses for a buffer or screen, space 3 to 6 feet or more apart, depending on the proposed maintained height.

CARE: When planted on drier sites, water as needed through periods of drought. Adding organic soils or mulches may also help keep the plant healthy. Trim as desired.

SITE CONDITIONS: Full sun to partial shade; moist to wet, well- or poorly drained acidic soils

HARDINESS: Zones 8A–10B

GARDEN TIPS: Dahoon holly is highly adaptable to a variety of conditions, from full sun to full shade and seasonally inundated to much drier soils (although supplemental irrigation may be necessary to establish). It can be used near ponds or wetland edges and other watercourses. It works well as an accent or specimen plant, as well as grouped and shaped to form a buffer or screen. The plant is dioecious, meaning male and female flowers are born on separate plants. Plants of both sexes are required if berries are desired, but only the female will produce fruit.

MARY KEIM

GALLBERRY
(Ilex glabra)

6–10 ft.

Gallberry is an evergreen shrub found in flatwoods, coastal swales, bogs, sinks, moist woodlands, and bayhead edges throughout Florida. Its tiny flowers attract bees, while its pulpy berries and evergreen foliage provide food and cover for birds.

Gallberry's flowers are greenish white with four to six rounded petals surrounding a bright green superior ovary. They are born in leaf axils either as single flowers (female) or in cymes (male or female). Leaves are ovate to elliptic, glossy, and dark green with pale green undersides. They are alternately arranged. Leaf margins are thick and may be entire, but are typically bluntly toothed or notched toward the leaf tip. Fruits are shiny black berries containing five to eight nutlets.

Native Americans dried, roasted, and steeped the leaves to make a black tea, giving the plant another common name: Appalachian tea. Honeybees feed on the flowers and produce a unique honey that is slow to crystallize due to its high pollen and enzyme content.

FAMILY: Aquifoliaceae (holly family)

NATIVE RANGE: Throughout Florida, excluding the Keys

LIFESPAN: Perennial

BLOOM SEASON: Spring

GROWTH HABIT: 6–10' tall; taller than wide

PROPAGATION: Division, seed. Clean seeds should be sowed quickly, although germination may take up to a year. Sprouts can be dug up and transplanted.

PLANTING: Plants are available in 1- and 3-gallon containers. Plant 3 feet apart in mass plantings.

CARE: Prune Gallberry to your desired size and shape. The plant sometimes develops leaf spot, especially during the wet season, but it is generally not a problem. Infected leaves may drop early.

SITE CONDITIONS: Full sun to partial shade; moist to very moist acidic, sandy soils

HARDINESS: Zones 8A–10B

GARDEN TIPS: Gallberry is clonal, spreading by underground rhizomes; however, it moves slowly and is easily controlled. It can be pruned to a desired shape, making it suitable for a screen or hedge planting. It also works well as a specimen plant or as part of a naturalistic landscape. The plant is dioecious, meaning male and female flowers are born on separate plants. Plants of both sexes are required if berries are desired.

CAUTION: Cultivars have been developed from plants found far north of Florida. These typically do not perform well in our state and will have only one sex.

SIDDARTH MACHADO

YAUPON HOLLY
(Ilex vomitoria)

6–20 ft.

Yaupon holly is an evergreen shrub or tree found in coastal and inland scrub, dunes, floodplains, and hammocks. Its diminutive flowers bloom in spring, attracting a variety of bees and other insects. In the fall, abundant fruit production provides food for birds and small mammals. The dense evergreen foliage provides year-round cover for wildlife.

Yaupon holly's flowers are small, white, and born in clusters within leaf axils. Simple leaves are oval to elliptic, dark green, and typically less than 1 inch long. They are leathery with crenate margins (unique for hollies) and have an alternate arrangement. Fruits are small (about ¼ inch in diameter) green berries that turn bright red when mature. Branches are gray and slender, and bark is smooth and whitish gray. The crown is densely branched.

Native Americans brewed a strong "black drink" (as it was known by early settlers) from Yaupon. Confederate soldiers used the tea as a substitute for coffee. In recent years, Yaupon holly tea has seen a revival and is available commercially. The plant is the only native North American species to contain caffeine and has more of it than coffee or green tea. The leaves and stems may be used fresh, dried, or roasted.

FAMILY: Aquifoliaceae (holly family)

NATIVE RANGE: Panhandle, peninsula south to Brevard, Highlands, and Sarasota counties

LIFESPAN: Perennial

BLOOM SEASON: Spring

GROWTH HABIT: 6–20'+ tall with crown spreading 5–10'+

PROPAGATION: Cuttings, seed

PLANTING: Plants are available in 1- to 65-gallon containers and field-grown specimens. Use as an accent plant or space plants 3 or more feet apart for masses in screens and buffers.

CARE: This plant is tough under many conditions and requires very little care. It may sucker and form a thicket, so periodic removal of unwanted sprouts may be necessary. Because of its small leaves and tight foliage, it is often sheared into balls or straight walls; however, this makes the plant less accessible to wildlife for food and shelter. If trimming is necessary, cut branches back to retain its wild and beautiful natural form.

SITE CONDITIONS: Full sun to partial shade; acidic to slightly alkaline, very moist to very dry, well-drained soils

HARDINESS: Zones 8A–9B

GARDEN TIPS: Yaupon holly works well as a specimen plant or in a buffer or screen. It tolerates salt and wind and is adaptable to many soil types. The plant is dioecious, which means both a male and female specimen are needed to ensure pollination and fruit.

CAUTION: This popular plant has a long history of many cultivars that were created within and beyond Florida. Those with a more natural, open form—such as the weeping variety—allow for wildlife usage. Dwarf and tightly sheared forms, often from male plants, will not produce fruit or allow for shelter. Cultivars also restrict genetic diversity.

YELLOW ANISE
(Illicium parviflorum)

10–20 ft.

Yellow anise is an evergreen shrub found in mesic hammocks, bluffs, ravines, and seepage swamps. It is endemic to only seven Central Florida counties. Its dense evergreen foliage provides cover for birds and other wildlife. Its lightly fragrant blooms appear in spring and summer.

Flowers are tiny (about ½ inch in diameter) with 12 to 15 greenish-yellow tepals. They are born on fleshy stalks. Leaves are up to 6 inches long, leathery, and elliptic with blunt tips. Margins are generally entire but may be undulate. The leaf's upper surface is dark green and smooth; the underside is flecked with pale glands. Leaf arrangement is alternate. Fruits are small green star-shaped capsules that turn brown and dehisce when mature, dispersing many seeds.

The entire plant—especially the leaves when crushed—emits an anise- or licorice-scented fragrance. It is related to the common spice Star anise (*Illicium verum*), but like many other anise species, including the Florida anise (*I. floridanum*) of North Florida, the leaves and fruit may be toxic. The bark is a source of anise oil, and the roots may be used like sassafras.

The genus name *Illicium* is from the Latin *illicio*, or "entice." The species epithet *parviflorum* is from the Latin *parvus*, meaning "small," and *flōs* (*flōris*), or "flower."

FAMILY: Schisandraceae (formerly Illiciaceae)

NATIVE RANGE: Marion, Volusia, Seminole, Lake, Orange, Polk, and Osceola counties

LIFESPAN: Perennial

BLOOM SEASON: Spring and summer

GROWTH HABIT: 10–20' tall with 5–10'+ spread

PROPAGATION: Cuttings, seed

PLANTING: When planting in masses, space 3 feet apart if mature plants will be trimmed or 6 feet apart if allowing plants to reach full height. A rich soil or soil amended with organic material will grow healthier plants and help protect the plant during periods of drought.

CARE: Keep adequately moist and prune according to need.

SITE CONDITIONS: Partial to full shade; moist to moderately dry, rich, acidic soils

HARDINESS: Zones 8A–10A

GARDEN TIPS: Yellow anise can be pruned to any desired shape, making it great for a buffer, screen, or hedge, or a specimen plant. Its foliage may thin when grown in full shade. The plant is relatively pest free but cannot tolerate salt or long periods of drought.

VIRGINIA WILLOW
(Itea virginica)

3–8 ft.

Virginia willow is an erect to spreading shrub with showy spikes of tiny white flowers that bloom late winter through spring. It occurs naturally in floodplain swamps, seepage slopes, and calcareous and mesic hammocks, and on stream and lake edges. The plant provides food and cover for wildlife.

Its inflorescence is a dense terminal spikelike raceme that droops downward. Individual flowers are star-shaped, with five white to pinkish petals and a five-lobed, cup-shaped calyx. Stamens are creamy white with pale pinkish anthers. Ovary and pistil are prominent. The dark green leathery leaves are elliptic to obovate with finely toothed margins and pointed tips. They are petiolate and alternately arranged. In the fall, leaf color changes to orange, red, burgundy, or purple. Plants generally become deciduous in Central and North Florida, remaining evergreen in South Florida. Branches are slender and arching. Seeds are born in inconspicuous brown capsules.

Despite its common name, Virginia willow is not a true willow, which are members of the *Salix* genus in the Salicaceae family. It is also known as Sweetspire and Tassel-white.

FAMILY: Iteaceae (sweetspire family)

NATIVE RANGE: Nearly throughout Florida, less in southernmost counties

LIFESPAN: Perennial

BLOOM SEASON: Late winter and spring

GROWTH HABIT: 3–8' tall with spread of up to 6'

PROPAGATION: Cuttings, seed

PLANTING: Plants are available in 1- and 3-gallon containers. Space 3 feet apart for mass plantings.

CARE: Occasional pruning and removal of suckers may be necessary, but it is not fast spreading. It has no serious pests, although it is chewed by some insects.

SITE CONDITIONS: Partial shade, but can sometimes tolerate full sun; moist to wet, poor to well-drained, acidic sandy, loamy, or clay soils. It is shorter with denser foliage in light shade and moist soil than in wetter, shadier sites.

HARDINESS: Zones 8A–10B

GARDEN TIPS: Virginia willow makes a lovely dense shrub and can provide year-round interest due to its attractive flowers, long bloom period, and fall color. Use it in mass or edge plantings, in naturalistic or restoration landscapes, and along retention ponds, streams, and other riparian zones where its suckering habit may help stabilize soil.

ELEANOR DIETRICH

BLACK IRONWOOD
(Krugiodendron ferreum)

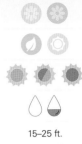

15–25 ft.

Black ironwood is a small evergreen tree found in tropical hammocks along Florida's central and southeast coast. Its fragrant flowers attract many pollinators, while its juicy berries provide food for birds and other wildlife. Humans can eat them, too, although they are best when made into a jelly or jam.

Black ironwood's flowers are small, yellowish green, and star-shaped. They are born in axillary clusters. Leaves are simple, oval to elliptic, and glossy with notched apices. Margins are entire and undulating, and leaf arrangement is opposite. Its bark is dark gray and rough; it may become furrowed with age. Fruits are small black drupes, each containing a single hard seed. They appear in summer and fall.

The genus name *Krugiodendron* honors German naturalist Karl Wilhelm Leopold Krug (1833-1898). The suffix *dendron* is Greek for "tree." The species epithet *ferreum* is from the Latin *ferreus*, or "iron," referring to the iron-like strength of the wood. It is thought to be the heaviest and densest wood of all trees native to North America and will sink in water. The plant also is known as Leadwood.

FAMILY: Rhamnaceae (buckthorn family)

NATIVE RANGE: East coast from Brevard County south to the Keys and Monroe County mainland

LIFESPAN: Perennial

BLOOM SEASON: Spring through late summer; year-round in South Florida

GROWTH HABIT: 15–25' tall; taller than wide

PROPAGATION: Clean seeds and sow quickly, as they do not store well.

PLANTING: This plant is available in 1- to 100-gallon containers and is widely cultivated. It is slow growing and should be placed in the landscape with that in mind.

CARE: Black ironwood is resistant to most pests and diseases. Once established, it generally needs little care.

SITE CONDITIONS: Full sun to full shade; dry to moist, well-drained sandy, loamy, or calcareous soils with some organic material

HARDINESS: Zones 10A–11A (may take temperatures to the upper 20s)

GARDEN TIPS: Black ironwood's dark leaves and gray to blackish bark provide a dramatic contrast when used as a background tree or shrub. It also works well as an accent or specimen tree. It is drought tolerant and moderately salt tolerant.

LEA KINDT

DOGHOBBLE
(Leucothoe axillaris)

2–4 ft.

Doghobble is an evergreen shrub found in swamps, wet hammocks, and flatwoods and along stream edges. Its profusion of spring-blooming flowers is pollinated primarily by bees.

Flowers are white to pinkish white, waxy, and urn- or bell-shaped. They are born in drooping axillary racemes. Calyces are five-lobed. The leaves are simple, leathery, and elliptic to lanceolate with pubescent petioles. The upper surfaces are dark green; undersides are lighter in color. Margins may be entire or have irregular serration. Leaf arrangement is alternate. Branches are loose and generally arching. The fruit is a round, dark brown capsule.

The genus name *Leucothoe* is from the Greek *leukós*, or "white," and alludes to the bloom color. The species epithet *axillaris* is from the Latin *axilla*, or "armpit," and references how the flowers are born in the leaf axils. According to legend, the common name "doghobble" originated with hunters whose dogs would become tangled in the plant's branches while chasing quarry.

FAMILY: Ericaceae (heath, azalea, or blueberry family)

NATIVE RANGE: Panhandle, some North and Central Florida counties

LIFESPAN: Perennial

BLOOM SEASON: Spring

GROWTH HABIT: 2–4' tall and spreading

PROPAGATION: Cuttings, seed (although not easily propagated by home gardeners)

PLANTING: Plants are available in 1- and 3-gallon containers. Space about 3 feet apart to allow for arching branches.

CARE: This plant needs no trimming or special care. A soil acidifier may be necessary.

SITE CONDITIONS: Partial to full shade; moderately moist to wet acidic soils

HARDINESS: Zones 8A–9B

GARDEN TIPS: Doghobble is best suited for moist, shady landscapes where little else will grow. It works well as a foundation plant in a north-facing spot and does especially well near a watercourse. Although the plant prefers shade, it will tolerate some sunlight. Its interesting dark evergreen foliage and showy flowers keep it attractive throughout the year.

CAUTION: Doghobble cultivars that are grown and sold outside of Florida may not perform well in Florida landscapes.

RYAN FESSENDEN

GOPHER APPLE
(Licania michauxii)

1 ft.

Gopher apple is a hardy, low growing, woody ground-cover that occurs naturally in sandhills, pine and scrubby flatwoods, scrub, coastal dunes, and pine rocklands. It typically blooms spring through summer but may bloom year-round, attracting a plethora of pollinators. Its fruit appears in late summer. It is edible to humans (although it is nearly tasteless) and other mammals but is a preferred food of gopher tortoises. The plant often is confused with Runner oak (*Q. pumila*), which has a similar growth habit and is found in similar habitats.

Gopher apple's flowers are small, creamy white, and born in erect terminal clusters. Leaves are leathery, stiff, and oblong. They can grow up to 4 inches long and are alternately arranged. Fruits are white drupes with a rosy blush, ovoid to ellipsoid in shape, and about 1 inch long or longer.

The species epithet *michauxii* pays homage to French botanist and explorer André Michaux (1746–1802), who is most noted for his study of North American flora. Some sources assign the botanical name *Geobalanus oblongifolius*.

FAMILY: Chrysobalanaceae (cocoplum family)

NATIVE RANGE: Throughout Florida

LIFESPAN: Perennial

BLOOM SEASON: Spring and summer; occasionally year-round

GROWTH HABIT: Up to 1' tall, rarely exhibiting aboveground branches; height may be greater near coastal areas

PROPAGATION: Seed. Clean and sow immediately after harvesting fruit.

PLANTING: Plants are available in quart and 1-gallon containers. To achieve a full groundcover more quickly, space plants as close as 2 feet apart.

CARE: Planted in deep sandy soils, Gopher apple requires no special care. New shoots appear in spring.

SITE CONDITIONS: Full sun; dry, well-drained sandy soils

HARDINESS: Zones 8A–11A

GARDEN TIPS: Gopher apple will spread and form colonies by way of underground rhizomes. It works well as a groundcover and can help stabilize soils. It is fire adapted and salt and drought tolerant.

ELEANOR DIETRICH

SHINY LYONIA
(Lyonia lucida)

3–8 ft.

Also known as Fetterbush (a common name for many species in this genus), Shiny lyonia (pictured, top) is a long-lived evergreen flowering shrub that occurs naturally in lower scrub edges, scrubby flatwoods, xeric hammocks, moist pine flatwoods, and forested wetlands. Flowers typically appear in spring and are attractive to butterflies and bees; fruits are eaten by birds and other wildlife. The foliage offers cover.

Shiny lyonia's small flowers are deep rose, pink, or white; urn- or bell-shaped; and born in clusters along branches. They have a pleasant honey-like fragrance. Leaves are bright green, leathery, and broadly elliptic with entire margins. A vein encircles the leaf margin, which is a helpful identifier. Leaves are alternately arranged, and bark is brownish gray. Fruit is a small oval capsule with very tiny seeds.

Its common descriptor "shiny" and its species epithet *lucida* refer to the shiny or bright leaf surface. *Lucida* is from the Latin *lucidus*, meaning "shining."

FAMILY: Ericaceae (heath, azalea, or blueberry family)

NATIVE RANGE: Throughout Florida, except Monroe County and the Keys

LIFESPAN: Perennial

BLOOM SEASON: Early spring

GROWTH HABIT: 3–8'+ tall and equally wide

PROPAGATION: Cuttings, seed. Use a mist bed to propagate cuttings.

PLANTING: Plants are available in 1- and 3-gallon containers. Space plants about 3 feet apart and water until well established.

CARE: Shiny lyonia has a fibrous root system near the surface, so a longer period is needed to establish. Growth is moderate and little pruning is needed to keep it to size, but it may benefit from shaping.

SITE CONDITIONS: Full sun to minimal shade; moist to moderately moist, acidic sandy, loamy, or clay soils with some organic material

HARDINESS: Zones 8A–10B

GARDEN TIPS: Shiny lyonia's bright green foliage has a fresh appearance that is accented by its many bell-shaped blooms that vary in color from plant to plant. Use in masses or mixed with other shrubs and grasses from a flatwoods ecosystem for a naturalistic landscape. The plant also can be used in masses next to a swamp edge. It can be temporarily inundated or tolerate short drought periods once established.

OTHER SPECIES: Rusty lyonia (*L. ferruginea*) (pictured, bottom) is very appealing for its rust-colored foliage and twisted trunk as it matures. This low-maintenance shrub is adaptable to very well-drained soils and is highly drought tolerant. Its size and irregular shape make it suitable as an accent plant and for naturalistic landscapes and border plantings. Staggerbush, or Fetterbush (*L. fruticosa*), also has rusty foliage and extends through South Florida but is not as readily available. It will grow in very well-drained moderately moist soils.

SOUTHERN MAGNOLIA
(Magnolia grandiflora)

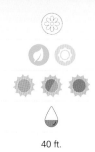

40 ft.

Southern magnolia is a majestic and iconic evergreen tree found in mesic hammocks and slope forests in North and Central Florida. It is renowned for its showy fragrant flowers, dramatic dark green leaves, and stately form. The flowers are primarily pollinated by beetles. Its abundant autumn fruits are eaten by small mammals, turkey, and quail.

Flowers are large (up to 12 inches in diameter), cuplike, and solitary. Petals are thick, creamy white, waxy, and number between 6 and 12 per flower. Blooms are highly aromatic, with a lemony or citronella-like scent. Leaves are broadly ovate and leathery with a shiny dark green upper surface and rust-colored underside. Leaves are alternately arranged and may be up to 10 inches long. The fuzzy, rose-colored fruit is a cone-shaped aggregate of drupe-like follicles. As the fruit ripens, the follicles turn bright red and shiny; they dangle from thin, threadlike filaments before falling.

Southern magnolia's leaves can be dried and used to season soups or stews. Its flower petals make a delicious condiment when pickled.

The genus name *Magnolia* pays homage to French botanist Pierre Magnol (1638–1715). The species epithet *grandiflora* means "large flower."

FAMILY: Magnoliaceae (magnolia family)

NATIVE RANGE: Panhandle, peninsula south to Highlands County

LIFESPAN: Perennial

BLOOM SEASON: Spring and summer

GROWTH HABIT: 40'+ tall with oval to pyramidal shape

PROPAGATION: Cuttings, seed

PLANTING: Trees are available from native plant nurseries in 3- to 100-gallon containers and field-grown specimens. Plant this accent tree where it can be truly appreciated and its fallen leaves are not an issue. See note below on cultivars.

CARE: Leaf litter can be a problem, as the leaves are slow to decompose. Some of the most graceful specimens have branches that bend and bow all the way to the ground, which helps reduce the problem of messy fallen leaves.

SITE CONDITIONS: Full sun to full shade; moist, well-drained sandy, clay, or loamy soils

HARDINESS: Zones 8A–9B

GARDEN TIPS: Southern magnolia is one of the most beautiful flowering trees. It adds elegance and charm to any landscape. It is moderately drought tolerant but can withstand brief periods of inundation. It is also hurricane resistant. Flowering is most prolific when planted in full sun. The tree's dense crown provides a deep shade, making it difficult to underplant.

CAUTION: It is estimated that there are well over 200 cultivars of this plant, and it is difficult to know where most have originated since the range of this species extends from North Carolina to Texas. Inquire with local growers as to which cultivars were developed from Florida native stock in your region. Non-cultivars are available from nurseries that specialize in native plants.

SIMPSON'S STOPPER
(Myrcianthes fragrans)

3–20 ft.

Also known as Twinberry, Simpson's stopper is an evergreen shrub or small tree that occurs naturally in coastal strands and hammocks. Its year-round blooms attract a variety of butterflies and bees, and its fruit provides food for many bird species, especially in summer. The sweet flesh of the fruit is edible to humans, but eating the bitter seeds is not recommended.

Each fragrant flower has four white petals and many long white stamens. They are born in clusters on paired stalks. Sepals are lobed and in fours. Leaves are bright green, ovate to elliptic, and leathery. They have entire margins and are oppositely arranged. Leaf surface is covered in small blackish dots. When crushed, leaves emit a citrus or pine aroma. Fruits are greenish ovoid berries that turn bright reddish orange as they mature. They are typically born in pairs, hence the common name "Twinberry." Bark is smooth, reddish brown, and flakes off in irregular shapes.

The common name "stopper" alludes to the plant's historical use as a treatment for diarrhea.

FAMILY: Myrtaceae (myrtle or eucalyptus family)

NATIVE RANGE: Coastal counties along the central and southern peninsula, St. Johns County, and the Keys

LIFESPAN: Perennial

BLOOM SEASON: Spring and summer; year-round in South Florida

GROWTH HABIT: 3–20'+ tall

PROPAGATION: Clean and sow seed without letting it dry out.

PLANTING: Plants are available in 1- to 30-gallon containers. Space 3 or more feet apart to use as a buffer or mass planting. It also does well as a specimen plant.

CARE: Allow the plant to reach mature form or prune to desired size. Its slow to moderate growth makes it easy to manage.

SITE CONDITIONS: Full sun to partial shade; dry to moist, sandy, neutral to slightly alkaline soils

HARDINESS: Zones 8A–11A

GARDEN TIPS: Simpson's stopper is an excellent ornamental plant with dense evergreen foliage; attractive, fragrant flowers; and colorful fruit. Despite its limited natural range, it can be adapted to well-drained landscapes into northern Florida, as it is quite cold tolerant. The plant is suitable for difficult areas where other plants may not do well. More sun exposure will contribute to a smaller form and will encourage more blooms. In the shade, Simpson's stopper may grow taller and have a more open, yet graceful, appearance.

KEITH BRADLEY

SLASH PINE
(Pinus elliottii)

50–100 ft.

A key element of Florida's ecology is the Slash pine, a fast-growing evergreen conifer found in scrub, scrubby flatwoods, flatwoods, rocky pinelands, and swamp edges. It provides vital food and habitat for small mammals, reptiles, and other wildlife and nesting cavities for birds. The flaky bark is good habitat for many insects, which in turn provide vital proteins for baby birds. Squirrels, in particular, enjoy stripping seeds from the cones to eat.

The needlelike leaves are glossy, dark green, and long (6 to 12 inches) with entire margins. They are alternately arranged, with two (sometimes three) leaves per fascicle. The trunk is typically straight. The crown is usually conical but may be round or flat. Seeds are winged and born in elongated (up to 6 inches) oval cones. Pollen is formed in catkins, or male pollen cones.

Two varieties occur in Florida: North Florida slash pine (*P. elliottii* var. *elliottii*) occurs throughout North Florida. The denser, slower-growing South Florida slash pine (*P. elliottii* var. *densa*) occurs from the center of the peninsula south. It tends to have a grass stage. Its buds are more crowded on the stem, and needles are more often in twos. South Florida slash pine tends to casually look more like Longleaf pine than the North Florida variety.

Most parts of pine trees are edible. The leaves have a piney or citrusy taste and can be made into a sun tea. Catkins are high in protein (although they have little flavor). The seeds (or "pine nuts") and inner bark also are edible.

The common descriptor "slash" comes from the slashes or cuts made in the tree to extract sap for turpentine. These "cat faces" can still be seen on old pines.

FAMILY: Pinaceae (pine family)

NATIVE RANGE: North Florida slash pine ranges from North into Central Florida. South Florida slash pine ranges from Central Florida into the Keys. Where they overlap, South Florida slash occurs in drier habitats.

LIFESPAN: Perennial

BLOOM SEASON: Although flowerless, pollen is dispersed winter through spring.

GROWTH HABIT: 50–100' tall; crown has 30'± spread. South Florida slash pine tends to be shorter.

PROPAGATION: Seed

PLANTING: Plants are available in 1- to 100-gallon containers and field grown. If planting in groups, space 5 to 10 feet or more apart. When shopping, specify whether North or South Florida slash pine is desired.

CARE: Fallen needles provide mulch.

SITE CONDITIONS: Full sun to partial shade; dry to moist, acidic, well-drained sandy, clay, or loamy soils

HARDINESS: Zones 8A–11A

GARDEN TIPS: Slash pine's fast growth rate makes it desirable as a specimen tree or for creating or enhancing a high pine canopy. It is moderately salt and highly drought tolerant.

CHICKASAW PLUM
(Prunus angustifolia)

12–20 ft.

Chickasaw plum is a deciduous flowering shrub or small tree that produces profuse blooms before leafing out, making for a spectacular spring display. It occurs naturally in dry hammocks, woodland edges, and disturbed areas and roadsides. The flowers are very attractive to a wide range of pollinators. The fruit is eaten by birds and other wildlife. Humans can eat it, too, but it is quite tart and has a large seed. It is best made into jelly.

Chickasaw flowers are five-petaled and white with many obvious yellow anthers. Blooms are cupped in yellowish-green sepals. Leaves are 1 to 2 inches long and lanceolate with shiny green surfaces and finely toothed margins. They are alternately arranged. Fruits are cherrylike yellow drupes that turn reddish when ripe, usually in late summer. Bark is rough and dark on the trunk but more reddish on branches. Chickasaw plum has an interesting growth habit that results in an irregular shape and a "twiggy" look.

The plums were a favorite food of Chickasaw Indians and other Native Americans who cultivated and spread the plant before Europeans arrived.

FAMILY: Rosaceae (rose family)

NATIVE RANGE: Central and west Panhandle, north and central peninsula

LIFESPAN: Perennial

BLOOM SEASON: Spring

GROWTH HABIT: 12–20' high and 10–20' wide

PROPAGATION: Cuttings, seed. Root cuttings or suckers may be moved, but digging may cause more suckering. Clean and cold-stratify the seed by placing moist seeds in the refrigerator for one to two months before sowing.

PLANTING: Plants are available in 1- to 15-gallon containers. Use as a specimen small tree or space 8 or more feet apart for masses.

CARE: Avoid soil disturbance, which is more likely to cause Chickasaw plum to sucker.

SITE CONDITIONS: Full sun to partial shade; dry to moist, sandy soils

HARDINESS: Zones 8A–9B

GARDEN TIPS: Because it has a tendency to sucker, Chickasaw plum can form dense thickets and may be difficult to control. This same characterization, however, also makes it a good candidate for a buffer or screen planting and for soil stabilization.

OTHER SPECIES: Flatwoods plum (*Prunus umbellata*) is a similar plant found in North and Central Florida sandhills and woods. It does not sucker, has a reddish-purple fruit, and is another usable landscape plant.

MARY KEIM

WILD COFFEE
(Psychotria nervosa)

1–8 ft.

Wild coffee is an evergreen shrub that occurs naturally in coastal, hydric, mesic, and rockland hammocks throughout Florida's peninsula. Its flowers typically bloom in spring and summer but may bloom year-round. They are attractive to a variety of pollinators, especially Atala and Schaus' swallowtail butterflies. The plant's fruits are a favorite of many birds and small wildlife. Humans can eat the berries as well, but they are rather bland. Unlike its cousin, *Coffea arabica*, from which our morning cup of joe is derived, Wild coffee fruit contains no caffeine. The seeds can be roasted and used as a caffeine-free coffee substitute but do so with caution, as some sources suggest the brew may induce a headache.

Wild coffee's many white to greenish-white flowers are small and tubular with four- or five-lobed calyces. They are born in sessile clusters that may be axillary or terminal. Its leaves are dark green, glossy, and obovate to elliptic with pointed apices, deep venation, and entire margins. They are oppositely arranged. Stems are glabrous. Fruits are oval drupes that turn bright red when ripe.

FAMILY: Rubiaceae (coffee, bedstraw, or madder family)

NATIVE RANGE: Peninsular Florida into the Keys

LIFESPAN: Perennial

BLOOM SEASON: Spring and summer

GROWTH HABIT: 1–8' tall with 1–5' spread; shorter in Central and North Florida

PROPAGATION: Clean and de-pulp seed before sowing.

PLANTING: Plants are available in 1- or 3-gallon containers. Space plants between 2 and 4 feet apart.

CARE: Wild coffee can easily be trimmed to any height and is relatively pest free.

SITE CONDITIONS: Partial to full shade; moderately dry to moist, well-drained sandy, loamy, or calcareous soils

HARDINESS: Zones 8B–11A

GARDEN TIPS: Wild coffee's beautiful evergreen foliage and low maintenance requirements make it a popular choice for many Florida landscapes. It can be used as a specimen or accent plant, although several planted together can form a loose understory or mass along shady edges. It is relatively salt tolerant and somewhat drought tolerant, but does not do well when exposed to too much sun or freezing temperatures. Wild coffee will produce more flowers and fruit in a partially shady site.

KEITH BRADLEY

Trees and Shrubs 🌿 **183**

JAMAICAN CAPER
(Quadrella jamaicensis)

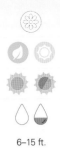

6–15 ft.

Jamaican caper is a handsome evergreen shrub or small tree with unique eye-catching blooms. These fragrant white flowers open late in the day and turn pinkish within a few hours. They attract a variety of insects, while the dense foliage provides cover for small wildlife. Birds will eat the seeds. Jamaican caper is a larval host for the Florida white butterfly. It is found in coastal hammocks in Central and South Florida.

The showy flowers are small (about 1 inch in diameter) with four notched petals. Most noticeable are the many conspicuously long filaments with pink or yellow anthers. The simple, dark green leaves are elliptic, leathery, and glossy with entire margins and scales underneath, giving them a whitish sheen. Fruits are tan pod-like capsules. When they open, they reveal a brilliant coral-colored endocarp and many shiny red to brown seeds. Young stems are covered in a rusty pubescence. The bark is rough and reddish brown. This large shrub to small tree is generally upright with an oval or pyramidal crown.

Taxonomically, Jamaican caper once was known as *Capparis cynophallophora*. Some sources still place it in the Capparaceae, or caper, family.

FAMILY: Brassicaceae (mustard, cabbage, or crucifer family)

NATIVE RANGE: Coastal counties from Brevard and Pinellas to the Keys

LIFESPAN: Perennial

BLOOM SEASON: Spring and summer

GROWTH HABIT: 6–15'+ tall and 6–10' wide

PROPAGATION: Seeds need to be scarified for germination.

PLANTING: Jamaican caper is widely cultivated in the south and can be purchased in 1- to 100-gallon containers or field grown. Place for a showy accent or space 3 to 5 feet apart. Some organic material will aid in growth.

CARE: No special care is needed for this evergreen, slow to moderate growing shrub, but it may be trimmed as needed.

SITE CONDITIONS: Full sun to partial shade; dry to moist, well-drained sandy or calcareous soils

HARDINESS: Zones 9B–11A

GARDEN TIPS: Jamaican caper is an excellent ornamental accent plant for both formal and naturalistic landscapes. It provides year-round interest with its dark shimmery foliage, beautiful spring blooms, and striking open seed pods. It works well as a specimen plant or en masse as a buffer or screen. It tolerates drought, salt, and hurricane winds and does very well as a coastal plant.

RYAN FESSENDEN

SAND LIVE OAK
(Quercus geminata)

20–30 ft.

Oaks are an essential plant for wildlife. They provide food and shelter and support many insects that also provide food for baby birds. Twenty-six oak species occur in Florida, most of which are grown commercially and will fill any landscape and climate need.

Sand live oak is an evergreen tree found in coastal hammocks, sandhills, scrub, and flatwoods throughout much of the state. It is highly valued by wildlife for both food and cover. Deer and rabbits may browse its young leaves and shoots. Its low-tannin acorns are an important food source for small mammals such as squirrels as well as some birds, especially the Florida scrub jay. The tree also is a larval host plant for several butterflies, including the Oak hairstreak and Red-banded hairstreak.

The leaves of Sand live oak are thick and leathery with coarse veins. The tops are dark green; the undersides and petioles are densely covered in a fine, gray to rust-colored pubescence (distinguishing it from Live oak). Leaf margins are revolute. Flowers are inconspicuous green catkins. Bark is dark, rough, and furrowed. Fruits are small (about 1 inch long) dark brown acorns that contain a single seed. They mature in late August and September and are generally animal-dispersed, resulting in many seedlings near and away from the parent tree.

FAMILY: Fagaceae (beech or oak family)

NATIVE RANGE: Throughout Florida, except southernmost counties

LIFESPAN: Perennial

BLOOM SEASON: Spring

GROWTH HABIT: 20–30'+ tall and as wide

PROPAGATION: Seed germinates readily, sometimes even while hanging from the tree.

PLANTING: Plants are readily available in 1- to 45-gallon containers or field grown. Place where shade is desired. Group three or more young trees close together to create an interesting trunk and branching arrangement over time.

CARE: Leaves drop just before leafing out in spring. Gather leaves and use for mulch elsewhere in the garden.

SITE CONDITIONS: Full sun to partial shade; dry, well-drained sandy or calcareous soils

HARDINESS: Zones 8A–10B

GARDEN TIPS: Sand live oak works well when a Live oak is desired but space is limited. It is smaller and grows at a slower pace than Live oak. It also is variable in its form and often grows in clusters in the wild.

OTHER SPECIES: Myrtle oak (*Q. myrtifolia*) is a smaller tree or shrub-like oak that occurs in dry, well-drained soils of coastal hammocks, scrub, sandhills, and flatwoods. Turkey oak (*Q. laevis*) is a sandhill and scrub species with larger, turkey-footed leaves that turn golden in winter. Bluejack oak (*Q. incana*) also occurs in deep, sandy soils. Its new spring leaves may be pink, blue, or light green. Live (*Q. virginiana*), Laurel (*Q. laurifolia*), and Water oak (*Q. nigra*) are larger shade trees suitable for moist to wet soils.

WHITE INDIGOBERRY
(Randia aculeata)

2–12 ft.

White indigoberry is an evergreen flowering shrub or small tree found in pine rocklands and coastal strands and hammocks in Central and South Florida. Its fragrant flowers bloom year-round, attracting a variety of butterflies, including Schaus' swallowtail. Its pulpy fruit provides food for many birds. The plant is the larval host plant for the Tantalus sphinx moth.

White indigoberry flowers are small, white, and five-lobed. They are born in the leaf axils. Leaves are orbicular with shiny upper surfaces and entire margins. They are oppositely arranged, often in terminal clusters. The plant's trunk and branches may be armed with thorns. Fruits begin as green, marble-sized berries. At maturity, they turn creamy white with dark bluish-black pulp (hence the plant's common name). The pulp has been used to make a blue dye.

The genus name *Randia* is an homage to English botanist Isaac Rand (1674–1743). The species epithet *aculeata* is from the Latin *acutus,* meaning "sharp" or "pointy," and refers to the thorny branches.

FAMILY: Rubiaceae (coffee, bedstraw, or madder family)

NATIVE RANGE: Coastal counties from Brevard County to the Keys and Pinellas and Hillsborough counties to mainland Monroe County

LIFESPAN: Perennial

BLOOM SEASON: Year-round

GROWTH HABIT: 2–12' tall and up to 6' wide (variable depending on growing conditions)

PROPAGATION: Seed. Remove pulp and sow with light covering of soil.

PLANTING: Plants are more commonly available in 3-gallon containers but are widely available in 1- to 30-gallon sizes.

Use as an accent plant or space about 3 feet apart.

CARE: This moderate- to slow growing plant is easy to keep in check. No other care is needed.

SITE CONDITIONS: Full sun to minimal shade; moist, well-drained calcareous or sandy soils

HARDINESS: Zones 10A–11A

GARDEN TIPS: White indigoberry is suitable for border, buffer, and hedge plantings. It also makes a nice specimen plant. Its evergreen leaves, stiff branches, and year-round blooms provide color and interest in the landscape. The plant is drought tolerant and does well in nutrient-poor soils.

DAMON MOORE

SWAMP AZALEA
(Rhododendron viscosum)

5–15 ft.

Swamp azalea is a long-lived deciduous shrub to small tree with fragrant, showy blooms. It occurs naturally in wet flatwoods, seep and bay swamps, and along lake margins. It flowers in midsummer and is attractive to a variety of pollinators, including hummingbirds. Swamp azalea is Florida's only white-flowered, summer-blooming rhododendron.

Flowers are white and may be tinged with pink. The long corolla is tubular and covered in sticky, gland-tipped hairs. It opens into five lobes, exposing five conspicuous stamens that extend well beyond the corolla. Leaves are simple and elliptic to oblong with a minute tooth at the apex. They are alternately arranged. Leaf margins are finely pubescent.

The genus name *Rhododendron* comes from the Greek *rhodon*, or "rose," and *dendron*, or "tree." The species epithet *viscosum* refers to the viscous glands on the corolla tube.

FAMILY: Ericaceae (heath, azalea, or blueberry family)

NATIVE RANGE: Panhandle, North and Central Florida

LIFESPAN: Perennial

BLOOM SEASON: Summer

GROWTH HABIT: 5–15' tall

PROPAGATION: Cuttings, seed

PLANTING: Plants are available in 1- and 3-gallon containers. Space about 3 feet apart. The plant has fibrous roots that sit close to the soil surface and takes a longer time to establish with frequent watering.

CARE: Water as needed through the spring drought period.

SITE CONDITIONS: Full sun to filtered shade (ideal); moist to wet, acidic soils rich in organics

HARDINESS: Zones 8A–9B

GARDEN TIPS: Although shade-adapted, Swamp azalea can tolerate sunlight and does well in canopied areas with light gaps and on edges where it receives dappled sunlight. It is not salt tolerant or drought tolerant unless planted in the right soils and well established.

OTHER SPECIES: Sweet pinxter azalea (*Rhododendron canescens*) is native to pine flatwoods, mesic hammocks, bay swamps, and floodplain and slope forests in the Panhandle and northern peninsula. It has showy pinkish to rose-colored trumpet-shaped flowers with noticeably protruding stamens and pistils. They bloom in early spring and have a sweet scent. Like all Florida native azaleas, it is deciduous. It does best in rich, acidic soils and full sun to partial shade. Use as a specimen plant, in a mass planting or naturalistic landscape, or in a container. Young plants may appear straggly but will fill in and spread out as they mature. Propagate by seed.

ELEANOR DIETRICH

SABAL PALM
(Sabal palmetto)

10–50 ft.

As one of our most ubiquitous native plants, it is easy to see why Sabal palm is Florida's state tree. Also known as Cabbage palm, this evergreen fan palm occurs nearly throughout Florida in pinelands, hammocks, coastal dunes, swamps, and floodplain forests. It provides significant food, shelter, and nesting material for many species of birds, mammals, reptiles, and amphibians. Its "boots" host a variety of ferns, some of which are threatened and endangered. It also is the larval host of the Monk skipper butterfly and other butterflies, and insects nectar on its flowers.

Flowers are tiny (less than ½ inch in diameter), creamy white, and born in long (up to 1 foot) compound panicles. Leaves are fanlike and deeply divided with smooth petioles. They are costapalmate, meaning they have an obvious midrib. Leaflets are many and often have threadlike filaments along the margins. The smooth petioles, midrib, and filaments are keys to differentiating a young Sabal palm from Saw palmetto (*Serenoa repens*). The trunk is generally straight (although it may be curved), unbranched, and often covered in remnant leaf bases, or "boots." Fruits are pea-sized, shiny, and black with a single seed.

Native Americans called it their "tree of life," using it for shelter and to make tools. Fiber was used to make netting, and the fronds were used for food and weaving baskets. Its edible terminal bud (or "heart") has a cabbage-like taste. Harvesting it, however, kills the tree and is highly discouraged.

FAMILY: Arecaceae (palm family)

NATIVE RANGE: Nearly throughout Florida

LIFESPAN: Perennial

BLOOM SEASON: Spring and summer

GROWTH HABIT: 10–50'+ tall

PROPAGATION: Seed (slow growing)

PLANTING: Plants are available in 1- to 10-gallon containers and field grown. They can be planted in almost any space large enough to accommodate the root ball. Place where falling fronds and fruits are not a problem. If planting in clumps, leave at least 4 feet between trees.

CARE: Sabal palms do not need their fronds trimmed; they are healthier if fronds are left to fall on their own.

Remember that green fronds supply the food for the tree and old fronds and fruit have much wildlife value. In the wild, some naturally lose their boots while others do not. Though generally free of disease, newly planted palms and established palms under stress may get bud rot. Call a professional for treatment.

SITE CONDITIONS: Full sun to partial shade; dry, moist, or seasonally wet sandy, loamy, or calcareous soils

HARDINESS: Zones 8A–11A

GARDEN TIPS: Sabal palm works well as a specimen tree in a variety of landscapes, as it is highly adaptable. It is a hardy, long-lived tree that is resistant to salt, hurricane winds, flood, fire, and drought. It is extremely slow growing except in wet locations.

LISA ROBERTS

CHAPMAN'S WILD SENSITIVE PLANT
(*Senna mexicana* var. *chapmanii*)

2–4 ft.

Chapman's wild sensitive plant is a robust evergreen perennial that occurs in pine rocklands and coastal strands and along hammock edges in Miami-Dade County and the Florida Keys. Because of its limited natural range, it is a state-listed threatened species. Its many flowers are visited by sweat, resin, cuckoo, leafcutter, and bumble bees for their pollen and nectar. Butterflies such as the Sleepy orange, Little yellow, Cloudless, Orange-barred, and Statira sulphurs are also frequent visitors. All members of the *Senna* genus are larval host plants for sulphur caterpillars.

The plant's flowers are born in stalked clusters. They have five buttery-yellow petals with subtle red venation. Each bloom has seven stamens with reddish anthers. Leaves are pinnately compound and alternately arranged. Leaflets are dark green and linear to elliptic with pointed tips. A gland at the base of the lowermost leaflets attracts ants that attack caterpillars. Stems are glabrous. Seeds are born in slender brown pods.

FAMILY: Fabaceae (legume, bean, or pea family)

NATIVE RANGE: Miami-Dade County and the Florida Keys

LIFESPAN: Perennial

BLOOM SEASON: Year-round

GROWTH HABIT: 2–4'+ tall and sprawling

PROPAGATION: Seed

PLANTING: Plants are available in 1- to 7-gallon containers. Use as a specimen shrub or in masses about 3 feet apart.

CARE: The plant may require occasional pruning if it gets too leggy. Removal of seed pods will help it remain attractive when not in flower and will decrease unwanted seedlings.

SITE CONDITIONS: Full sun to minimal shade; dry to slightly moist, well-drained calcareous soils

HARDINESS: Zones 10A–11A

GARDEN TIPS: Despite its limited natural range, Chapman's wild sensitive plant can be planted in landscapes as far north as Central Florida. It is drought but not cold tolerant and may die if exposed to below-freezing temperatures. Chapman's wild sensitive plant grows quickly and will self-seed. Interesting foliage and bright, showy flowers that bloom year-round make it a great ornamental specimen.

CAUTION: Many nonnative *Senna* species are sold commercially. In particular, Christmas senna (*S. pendula*), or Butterfly senna, is often recommended for butterfly gardens. However, the Florida Exotic Pest Plant Council (FLEPPC) lists it as a Category I invasive species known to alter native plant communities. It should be avoided.

SAW PALMETTO
(Serenoa repens)

3–6 ft.

Saw palmetto is an evergreen shrub found in scrub, pine-lands, coastal hammocks, and dunes in all but mainland Monroe County. Dr. Mark Deyrup of Archbold Biological Station calls it the "most amazing plant in Florida." He has counted 311 species that use Saw palmetto, while many other species have documented interlocking relationships with the plant. It is extremely valuable to hundreds of species of birds, mammals, and other wildlife and insects as a source of food and cover. Its flowers are a major source of nectar for honeybees. Its berries are a staple for the Florida black bear. They also are edible to humans.

Flowers are tiny (less than ¼ inch in diameter), creamy white, and born in long, dense panicles. They have a subtle but sweet fragrance. Leaves are fanlike and deeply divided, with 20± leaflets and a thick petiole that is armed with tiny but sharp teeth (hence the common name). Trunks may be upright but are generally prostrate or underground. Bark is fibrous. Fruits are oblong orangish-yellow drupes that turn black when ripe.

A silver form of Saw palmetto is found frequently near Florida's east coast. Its leaves have a waxy coating that gives them a silver hue.

The genus name *Serenoa* pays homage to American botanist Sereno Watson (1826–1892). The species epithet *repens* is Latin for "creeping" and refers to the low, creeping habit of the trunk.

FAMILY: Arecaceae (palm family)

NATIVE RANGE: Throughout Florida, except mainland Monroe County

LIFESPAN: Perennial

BLOOM SEASON: Spring

GROWTH HABIT: 3–6'+ tall and as wide

PROPAGATION: Seed can be cleaned and sown. Uncleaned seeds can be used, but the fruits may be more attractive to wildlife.

PLANTING: Plants are available in 1- to 30-gallon containers and field grown. Plant alone or in masses 3 to 5 feet apart, or mixed with grasses and wild-flowers as in a natural ecosystem.

CARE: This slow growing palm is easy to establish and will increase in size quickly when planted from containers.

SITE CONDITIONS: Full sun to partial shade; dry to moist sandy, loamy, or calcareous soils. Saw palmetto usually grows only to the edges of wetlands.

HARDINESS: Zones 8A–11A

GARDEN TIPS: Saw palmetto is a slow growing and long-lived plant. It works well as a specimen or accent shrub, or can be grouped to form a low buffer, particularly in areas where foot traffic is not desired. It is fire dependent, meaning it usually requires fire to stimulate flower and seed production. It is highly tolerant of drought and moderately so of salt winds.

CAUTION: The petiole teeth are extremely sharp. Care should be taken when handling this plant. It is not recommended for areas where children may play.

YELLOW NECKLACEPOD
(Sophora tomentosa var. truncata)

4–10 ft.

Yellow necklacepod is a long-lived flowering shrub that occurs naturally in coastal strands, hammocks, and dunes throughout Central and South Florida. The flowers, which bloom year-round, attract butterflies, bees, hummingbirds, and other small birds. The plant provides food and cover for a variety of wildlife.

Yellow necklacepod's bright yellow flowers are typical of the pea family—irregularly shaped with a broad upper petal (banner) and two adjacent petals (wings) surrounding fused bottom petals that form a boatlike structure called a keel. The flowers are born in long (6 to 12 inches) terminal racemes. Leaves are pinnately compound and alternately arranged. Leaflets, which number as many as 21 per leaf, are thick, ovate to elliptic, and oppositely arranged. Young leaflets (as well as the trunk and stems) are slightly hairy and may become glabrous as they mature. Fruits are stalked pods up to 6 inches long with severe constrictions around each seed compartment, resembling a beaded necklace (hence the common name). Seeds are round, yellowish brown, and poisonous.

FAMILY: Fabaceae (legume, bean, or pea family)

NATIVE RANGE: Coastal counties of Central and South Florida

LIFESPAN: Perennial

BLOOM SEASON: Year-round

GROWTH HABIT: 4–10'+ tall with 4–8' spread

PROPAGATION: Seed (see caution below)

PLANTING: Available in 1- to 7-gallon containers. Yellow necklacepod can be planted as a specimen or in masses; space 4 or more feet apart to allow for spread.

CARE: Plants can be pruned easily to size and shape desired. Pods may be removed, but they do add an interesting feature to the garden with their long, drooping character.

SITE CONDITIONS: Full sun; dry to moist, well-drained sandy or calcareous soils

HARDINESS: Zones 9A–11A

GARDEN TIPS: Yellow necklacepod is a fast-growing, hardy plant with interesting foliage, flowers, and seeds. It tolerates drought and salt but cannot withstand freezing temperatures.

CAUTION: *Sophora tomentosa* var. *truncata* is often confused with the nonnative *S. tomentosa* var. *occidentalis*, which is often sold in big-box store garden centers. The latter can be distinguished by the many fine hairs that cover it. The two species can cross-pollinate, so care should be taken to avoid the nonnative variety as well as seeds that may have been cross-pollinated. Both are known by the common name of Yellow necklacepod and both bear poisonous seeds.

KEITH BRADLEY

DARROW'S BLUEBERRY
(Vaccinium darrowii)

1–2 ft.

Darrow's blueberry is a small evergreen shrub that is under-appreciated as a landscape plant. Its profuse blooms appear in spring, attracting a variety of pollinators, particularly native bees. The sweet, juicy berries that follow in the summer are attractive to birds and other wildlife, as well as humans. Plants occur naturally in pine and scrubby flatwoods and sandhills throughout much of Florida.

The many white to whitish-pink flowers are small (less than ½ inch), urn-shaped, and born in dangling clusters. The flowers are cupped in conspicuous sepals that vary from green to dark pink. Leaves are simple and lanceolate to ovate with entire (occasionally revolute) margins. A glaucous coating gives the leaves a bluish-green or silvery hue. Leaf arrangement is alternate. The shrub is densely branched. Fruits are round, dark blue berries with a glaucous surface.

FAMILY: Ericaceae (heath, azalea, or blueberry family)

NATIVE RANGE: Nearly throughout Florida, except some southeastern and northeastern counties

LIFESPAN: Perennial

BLOOM SEASON: Spring

GROWTH HABIT: 1–2'+ tall and equally wide

PROPAGATION: Cuttings, division, seed

PLANTING: Plants are available in 1- and 3-gallon containers. Space about 2 feet apart in masses or mixed with Shiny blueberry (*V. myrsinites*). Plant where soil is naturally acidic, add composted material, or use an acidifier. Plant away from new sidewalks and other concrete sources that may leach and make the soil more alkaline. The fine surface-growing roots of Darrow's blueberry take longer to establish.

CARE: After plants are well established, they should not need additional watering except in long droughts. They will spread via underground stems to form colonies, but they expand slowly and are easy to control. This dense subshrub rarely needs pruning.

SITE CONDITIONS: Full sun to partial shade; dry to seasonally wet, well-drained, acidic sandy soils

HARDINESS: Zones 8A–10A

GARDEN TIPS: Use Darrow's blueberry as a low border planting, in masses, or as a specimen or accent plant. Its beautiful and interesting foliage, copious blooms, and showy fruit provide interest year-round. It is hardy, adaptable, and drought tolerant.

OTHER SPECIES: Shiny blueberry is similar to and often grows with Darrow's blueberry in intermixed colonies. Its young leaves are shiny with black dots or glands on the backs. Its range extends into Florida's southeastern and northeastern counties. Highbush blueberry (*V. corymbosum*) occurs in wetter and shadier locales throughout Central and North Florida. It sometimes interbreeds naturally with Darrow's blueberry. Both Darrow's and Highbush blueberry have been used to develop the Florida commercial cultivars of our growing blueberry industry.

WALTER'S VIBURNUM
(Viburnum obovatum)

2–12 ft.

Walter's viburnum is an evergreen woody shrub to small tree that occurs naturally in flatwoods, hydric hammocks, riverine forests, floodplain swamps, and bottomland forests. Pollinators are attracted to its showy spring flower clusters, while birds and other wildlife feast on its abundant summer and fall fruit production and use its dense foliage for nesting and cover.

Walter's viburnum has dainty white flowers born in flat-topped clusters. Its leaves are small (about 1 inch in length), ovate to spatulate, and oppositely arranged. They are dark green and leathery and may have either entire or slightly toothed margins. The fruit is a flat red drupe that turns black when mature.

This species was previously placed in the Caprifoliaceae (honeysuckle) family.

FAMILY: Adoxaceae (moschatel family)

NATIVE RANGE: Throughout Florida, except the Keys

LIFESPAN: Perennial

BLOOM SEASON: Spring

GROWTH HABIT: Variable, up to 12' and as wide

PROPAGATION: Cuttings, seed. Cuttings are the most reliable propagation technique. Seeds require stratification before planting.

PLANTING: Space 3 or more feet apart depending on its intended use.

CARE: The natural form is very graceful; however, plants may be pruned to a preferred shape and height.

SITE CONDITIONS: Full sun to full shade; moist to wet, fertile sandy, clay, or calcareous soils

HARDINESS: Zones 8A–10A

GARDEN TIPS: Walter's viburnum is an excellent choice as an accent plant, both for its form and its early spring flowers. It also makes a great hedgerow or border/screen plant and can be planted in masses. Plants can send up suckers, but they can be kept in check with timely pruning. It is moderately fast growing, extremely adaptable to a broad range of conditions, and is hurricane wind resistant. Walter's viburnum may experience a brief deciduous period in North Florida and/or in colder winter temperatures.

CAUTION: Most cultivars have been developed outside of the state and do not perform well in Florida landscapes. Some, including Riefler's dwarf and Mrs. Shiller's delight (both developed in Florida), widen the usability in home landscapes, but caution is still advised, as the genetic diversity may be compromised with the use of clones.

MARY KEIM

ADAM'S NEEDLE
(Yucca filamentosa)

6 ft.

Adam's needle is a low growing evergreen shrub found in scrub, sandhills, flatwoods, and coastal dunes throughout much of Florida. As a landscape plant, it provides interest with its unique swordlike leaves and striking flowers. The blooms are frequented for their nectar by hummingbirds and butterflies such as the Great southern white. It is pollinated in part by the Yucca moth and is a larval host plant for the Cofaqui and Yucca giant skipper butterflies.

The showy white flowers are born in large (2 to 5 feet tall) terminal panicles. Individual blooms are six-parted, bell-shaped, and droop downward. They are often tinged with purple. Basal leaves are long (2 to 4 feet), lanceolate, and arching with sharp pointed tips. Margins are entire with many fibrous filaments. Leaf veination is parallel. Stem leaves and trunk are generally absent. Taproot is large and fleshy with many lateral roots. Seeds are born in green capsules that turn black when ripe.

Some sources place this species in the Agavoideae subfamily of the Asparagaceae family. Although parts of *Yucca filamentosa* are edible, this plant is not related to the culinary plant, yuca, which is another name for Cassava (*Manihot esculenta*).

FAMILY: Agavaceae (agave family)

NATIVE RANGE: Nearly throughout Florida, except southernmost counties

LIFESPAN: Perennial

BLOOM SEASON: Spring

GROWTH HABIT: 2–3' tall; 6'± when in bloom

PROPAGATION: Division, seed. Collect in midsummer when the seed stalks have matured. Pups will develop next to the main plant and can easily be transplanted to another site.

PLANTING: Plants are readily available from native plant nurseries in 1- and 3-gallon containers. Space plants 30 to 36 inches apart to allow room for them to stand out and for airflow. Plant in deep sandy soils with no mulch for best results.

CARE: Dead leaves may be removed.

SITE CONDITIONS: Full sun to minimal shade; dry to moderately moist, well-drained, acidic to near neutral sandy soils

HARDINESS: Zones 8A–10B

GARDEN TIPS: The distinct foliage and flowers of Adam's needle make it a nice accent plant either as an individual specimen or in a group. It is tolerant of drought but has a low tolerance of salt winds.

CAUTION: Because of its sharply tipped leaves, Adam's needle is not recommended for areas where children may play.

COONTIE
(Zamia integrifolia)

1–4 ft.

Coontie is a small to medium evergreen cycad native to pine rocklands, hammocks, and pinelands throughout peninsular Florida. It is the only cycad native to North America. Coontie is the larval host for the Atala butterfly, which was once thought to have become extinct in Florida. Its recovery can be attributed to the increased use of Coontie in residential and commercial landscapes.

Coontie's fernlike leaves have a central stalk and many stiff, linear leaflets that are oppositely arranged. Male pollen cones are erect, dark brown, and narrowly cylindrical, born in clusters of two to five. Female cones are broadly ovoid and woody. As the cone matures, it splits open to reveal many large (about 1 inch long), salmon-pink seeds that turn bright orange and fleshy as they ripen. Fruit matures in fall and winter. The trunk is generally subterranean. Roots are tuberous.

Coontie is considered commercially exploited in Florida, meaning it has been removed in large numbers from natural areas to be sold. Collecting Coonties without a permit is illegal.

FAMILY: Zamiaceae (a cycad family)

NATIVE RANGE: Most peninsular counties and the Keys

LIFESPAN: Perennial

GROWTH HABIT: 1–4' tall and equally wide

PROPAGATION: Division, seed. To ensure germination, remove the fleshy covering from at least the pointed end of the seed where new growth will emerge.

PLANTING: Coontie is available in 1- to 3-gallon containers and larger. Space plants 2 to 3 feet apart. More distance gives better airflow; however, also consider that the plant is slow growing.

CARE: Coontie is highly adaptable and easy to care for once established. It is susceptible to scale and mold. If infected, cut back to the ground; it will regenerate. Good airflow around the plant will help keep these pests at bay.

SITE CONDITIONS: Full sun to full shade; dry to moist, well-drained sandy or calcareous soils

HARDINESS: Zones 8A–11A

GARDEN TIPS: This tough cycad can be planted almost anywhere, including along walkways, parking areas, or wherever it is adjacent to concrete or in acidic soils. Its low growing habit makes it well-suited for a border or mass planting or accent shrub. It tolerates salt, drought, and cold (although it may die back if exposed to freezing temperatures). It is a prolific self-seeder, with seedlings often sprouting in proximity to the parent plant. The plant is dioecious, meaning male and female seeds are born on separate plants.

WILD LIME
(Zanthoxylum fagara)

5–20 ft.

Wild lime is an evergreen shrub to small tree that occurs naturally in hammocks throughout Central and South Florida. It blooms year-round, with peak flowering in winter and spring. Its dense foliage provides cover, and its fruit provides food for birds and small wildlife. The plant is the larval host for several butterflies, including Giant and Schaus' swallowtails.

Wild lime flowers are tiny and yellow to yellowish green. They are born in clusters that emerge from the leaf axils. Leaves are pinnately compound with a winged midrib. They are alternately arranged. Leaflets are shiny, short (1 to 2 inches long), and obovate with crenate margins. Round, yellowish-green fruits mature into a dark brown husk that splits to reveal one or two shiny black seeds. The plant's trunk and branches are armed with hooked thorns, and its bark is scaly.

Despite its common name, Wild lime is merely a cousin of culinary limes and other citrus fruit. It is also known as Lime prickly ash, although it is not related to ash trees. Wild lime flowers and crushed leaves smell like lime. The leaves and bark can be ground into a powder and used as a bitter spice.

FAMILY: Rutaceae (rue or citrus family)

NATIVE RANGE: Peninsula from Marion County south to the Keys

LIFESPAN: Perennial

BLOOM SEASON: Year-round, peaking in winter and spring

GROWTH HABIT: 5–20'+ tall and 3–10' wide

PROPAGATION: Seed

PLANTING: Plant about 5 feet apart in a location where its thorniness is welcome.

CARE: Allow Wild lime to attain its natural shape or prune to fit tighter spaces. Except for the butterfly larvae that will munch on it, it is pest free.

SITE CONDITIONS: Full sun to partial shade; very dry to moist, well-drained sandy, loamy, or calcareous soils

HARDINESS: Zones 9A–11A

GARDEN TIPS: Wild lime is suitable for both formal and naturalistic landscapes. With its dense foliage and thorny branches, it is a great choice for establishing a buffer or privacy screen. The plant can tolerate partial shade, but when grown in full sun, it produces a fuller crown and many more blooms. It is easy to establish, adaptable to a variety of conditions, and grows fairly quickly. It is also moderately salt and drought tolerant. The plant is dioecious, which means both a male and female specimen are needed to ensure pollination and fruit. Only the females will produce fruit.

GLOSSARY OF HELPFUL TERMS

achene: a dry, indehiscent, one-seeded fruit.

acicular: slender or needle-shaped.

annual: a plant that germinates, flowers, sets seed, and dies within one year.

anther: the pollen-bearing part of the stamen.

apex (pl. apices): the tip or point farthest from the point of attachment.

appressed: pressed closely but not fused (e.g., leaves against a stem).

awn: a narrow bristlelike appendage.

axil: the angle formed between one plant and another (e.g., stem and leaf).

axillary: arising from or born in the leaf axil.

basal: forming or attached at the base.

bract: a modified leaf occurring at the base of a flower or inflorescence.

calcareous: a type of soil containing calcium carbonate; generally associated with limestone.

calyx (pl. calyces): the sepals of a flower, typically forming a whorl that encloses the petals and protects the flower bud.

capsule: a dry fruit composed of two or more carpels.

carpel: the female reproductive part of a flower, consisting of an ovary, stigma, and (usually) style.

caryopsis: a dry, indehiscent, one-seeded fruit with the seed coat closely fused to the fruit wall; typical of grasses.

catkin: a dense, pendulous, flowering spike.

cordate: heart-shaped.

corm: a fleshy underground stem.

corolla: collective term for all the petals of a flower.

corona: petal- or crown-like structure between the petals and stamens of a flower, often united in a tube.

corymb (adj. corymbose): a type of inflorescence with lower stalks proportionally longer than upper stalks so that the flowers form a flat or slightly rounded head.

crenate: having blunt or scalloped teeth.

cultivar: a horticultural variety of a naturally occurring "wild" plant species that was produced in cultivation by selection.

cypsela: a dry, indehiscent, one-seeded fruit

cyme (adj. cymose): a type of inflorescence with the main axis and all lateral branches ending in a flower.

deciduous: not persistent, seasonally falling off (e.g., leaves falling from a tree); compare with evergreen.

dehiscent: opening at maturity or when ripe (e.g., fruit to release seed).

disk floret: in flowers of the Asteraceae family, the tubular-shaped florets that form the "eye," or center of the bloom; compare with ray floret.

drupe: a fleshy fruit formed from a single carpel, with seed encased in a stony endocarp.

ecotype: a distinct form of a plant species that occupies a particular habitat.

endemic: having a natural range restricted to a specific geographic region.

endocarp: the innermost layer of a fruit wall.

entire: smooth; not toothed, lobed, or divided.

evergreen: having persistent green leaves; compare with deciduous.

fascicle: a tight bundle, cluster, or tuft (usually leaves).

filament: the stalk of the stamen that supports the anther; a threadlike structure.

follicle: a dry, dehiscent fruit formed from a single carpel and opening along a single suture to which the seeds are attached (e.g., milkweed pod).

glabrous: smooth; lacking surface hairs or scales.

glaucous: covered with a whitish, bluish, or silvery waxy coating.

herbaceous: not woody.

hybrid (adj. hybridize): a plant produced by crossing parent plants of different species, subspecies, or varieties.

hydric: wet; a habitat that is consistently very moist to very wet.

indehiscent: not opening at maturity along any definite line, pore, or suture (e.g., fruit such as a peach, apple, or cherry).

inflorescence: the flowering part of a plant; a cluster of flowers or florets.

internode: the portion of a stem between two nodes.

involucre: a whorl of bracts surrounding an inflorescence at its base.

keel: a ridgelike structure resembling the keel of a boat, formed by the fusion of two petals in flowers of the Fabaceae family.

leaflet: each of the leaflike structures that together make up a compound leaf.

margin: the edge (e.g., leaf edge).

mesic: a habitat that is moderately moist.

nutlet: a small nut; one of the sections of the mature ovary of some members of the Boraginaceae, Lamiaceae, and Verbenaceae families.

ovary: the basal portion of a carpel that contains the ovules.

panicle: a type of inflorescence consisting of a loose, branching cluster of flowers.

pappus: a tuft of hairs, awns, or bristles on a fruit or seed.

perennial: a plant whose life extends over several years.

petal: an individual member or segment of the corolla, usually soft and colored.

petiole (adj. petiolate): a leaf stalk.

pinnate: a feather-like compound leaf with leaflets arranged on opposite sides of an elongated petiole.

pistil: the female reproductive organs of a flower, generally consisting of a stigma, style, and ovary.

prostrate: lying flat on the ground.

pubescent: covered in soft, short hairs.

punctate: dotted with pits, glands, or colored dots.

raceme: an elongated, unbranched inflorescence with flowers that mature from the bottom up.

rachis: the main axis of a leaf or inflorescence.

ray floret: in flowers of the Asteraceae family, the strap-shaped, petal-like florets that form the ray of the bloom; compare with disk floret.

revolute: rolled under, downward, or backward.

rhizome (adj. rhizomatous): a perennial underground stem that grows horizontally.

rosette: a dense, radiating cluster of leaves, usually growing close to the ground.

sagittate: shaped like an arrowhead.

samara: a dry, indehiscent, winged fruit.

schizocarp: a dry, indehiscent fruit that splits into separate one-seeded segments at maturity.

sepal: an individual member or segment of the calyx, usually green.

serrate: having a sawlike edge; toothed.

sessile: attached without a stalk or petiole.

sheath: a tubular or rolled part of an organ that covers another organ (e.g., the leaf base of a grass forms a sheath around the stem).

simple: undivided or unsegmented (e.g., a leaf that is not divided into leaflets).

spatulate: spoon- or spatula-shaped.

stamen: the male organ of a flower, generally consisting of a filament and anther.

style: part of the pistil that connects the stigma to the ovary.

subspecies: a taxonomic rank below species that identifies geographic or morphological differences within a species.

taproot: the primary root from which smaller root branches arise.

tendril: a thin, threadlike appendage used by climbing plants to grasp an object (primarily another plant) for support.

tepal: a segment of a flower that is indistinguishable as either sepal or petal.

terminal: occurring at the tip or apex.

umbel (adj. umbellate): a type of inflorescence in which flower stalks are equal in length and emerge from a single point, like the struts of an umbrella, to form a flat or rounded head.

variety: a taxonomic rank below subspecies that identifies differences within a species.

whorl: a ringlike arrangement of leaves, bracts, or floral parts.

INDEX

ABOUT THE AUTHORS

Stacey Matrazzo joined the Florida Wildflower Foundation staff in 2015 as its program manager after serving several years as a contractor. She is an environmental educator and adjunct professor at Rollins College, Winter Park. Stacey is a certified Florida Master Naturalist who holds a bachelor's degree in Environmental Studies and a master's degree in Liberal Studies from Rollins. She has compiled more than 250 native wildflower species for the foundation's popular weekly social media/online feature, "Flower Friday." A native Floridian, she spends much of her free time kayaking, hiking, birding, and photographing Florida's amazing natural environments.

Nancy Bissett is a horticulturist, restoration ecologist, and botanist with The Natives Inc., a Davenport, Florida, firm offering consulting, ecological restoration, and landscape architecture services. At The Natives' nursery, she has experimented with the propagation and growth of many native plants, including grasses, wildflowers, and rare species. Nancy, who serves on the Florida Wildflower Foundation board, developed many restoration techniques for upland communities while working on projects for state agencies, water management districts, mitigation banks, mined lands, developers, and corporations throughout Florida. She has assisted with monitoring research projects for The Nature Conservancy, the Florida Fish and Wildlife Conservation Commission, and others, and she has performed rare plant and vegetation surveys and helped federal, state, and local authorities find and evaluate rare plant communities.

ABOUT THE FLORIDA WILDFLOWER FOUNDATION

The nonprofit Florida Wildflower Foundation is the national advocate for the state's native wildflower species, many of which occur throughout the Southeast. The organization nurtures the awareness, understanding, and enjoyment of Florida's native wildflowers and plants through projects that increase the presence of wildflowers and support the wildlife depending upon them. Visit www.flawildflowers.org to download resources, view grant opportunities, and learn more about its work.

FLORIDA
WILDFLOWER
FOUNDATION